INDEX

FOREWARD

BY: TONY GREENLAND

As I approach my seventieth Birthday I feel honored that not only that I should be remembered by Adam, but that I should also write the forward to his publication(s)

It was some twenty years ago that from writing articles in modelling magazines around the world I was asked to write a book with the rather grandiose title "Panzer Modelling Masterclass". At this time I believed it was generally well received and I made an attempt to cover all facets of modelling a tank (be it always a German WWII model!). My emphasis was very much on Kit Improvement and alterations to produce as accurate a kit in all aspects. From construction, decals, painting to the theater of operations.

The overriding necessity to improve the kit slowly became redundant as the likes of Dragon, Trumpeter, AFV club, etc , etc began releasing highly accurate kits. To me the painting was but one of the stages in production. All too often when criticized for too "pretty" a model I used the excuse of "the model represents the actual vehicle and not the Battle or Country it fought in". The book was successful if the reviews are to be believed, but, one would need to be very conceited to believe that the zenith had been reached. If you write a book

about techniques (…on any subject) there will always be someone out there that reads your work and who will pick up the baton and improve upon what you may have considered as your unique technique.

Since those halcyon days of the 1990's I have observed a distinct change in the emphasis in the AFV modelling world. There are a substantial number of highly talented finishers of these high quality kits. The emphasis has changed from construction to finishing. The quality of the kits and the finishing is breathtaking in their realism. A consequence of these finishing styles is the plethora of paints/pigments available to the modeller that bring such realism to their model. With these products are a large number of publications on "how to do". Why are these two volumes from Adam different from other publications? Well, together they cover the full spectrum of modelling AFV's. Every aspect of modelling AFV's is treated in a professional, readable and easily understood manner. The purchase of these two publications would provide a lifetime of information to build and improve upon even the most talented modeller, no longer just the finishing but all aspect of construction to completion.

01 ARMOUR MODELLING

BY ADAM WILDER
FOR JEFF, GAIL, RYAN, TAMMY AND JENIECE WILDER

ACKNOWLEDGMENTS

THE FOLLOWING HAVE CONTRIBUTED, ADVISED AND ENCOURAGED ME DURING THE MAKING OF THESE TWO BOOKS:

I would like to thank Thomas Anderson and Daniele Guglielmi for the historical photos. I would also like to express my gratitude to Sven Frisch along with Gail and Jeff Wilder for their continual counsel and also helping with the text of this book. Jari Hemila for the step-by-step photos in the segment about Applying Markings and Insignia is also much appreciated. I would like to thank Sven Frisch, Harry Steinmüller and

Scott Negron for the information and assistance with the Zimmerit Chapter. Thanks to the people at Lifecolor, Valljo Acrylics and Aber for the consumables and parts needed to finish the models seen throughout these pages. Finally, I would like to thank Ivan Cocker, César Oliva and Calvin Tan for the wonderful figures seen on the AFVs throughout these two books.

I WOULD ALSO LIKE TO THANK THE FOLLOWING FOR THEIR ADVICE AND SUPPORT THROUGHOUT THIS PROJECT:

David Parker
Keith Smith
Rodion Zotov
Maxim Chekanov, aka: Comanche75
Andrew Beletz
Francois Verdier

Zack Sex
Jim Galante
Vladimir Yashin
Karl Logan
.

INTRODUCTION

THESE TWO BOOKS ARE A PROJECT THAT I HAVE BEEN PUTTING TOGETHER FOR SOME TIME.

They are a culmination of everything that I have learned, studied and taught myself about building and painting armour models. There are many step-by-step photos to aid in the explanation of the methods covered. It is important that you also read the text in order to obtain a good understanding of the various techniques that I explain. Most seasoned modellers who publish agree that people do not always devote the time to carefully read the text focusing only on the photos. As a result they do not always obtain all of the information available to them.

These two books cover in detail the construction and painting phases in order performed by myself and many other modellers throughout the completion of a scale armour model. The first one includes examples of everything from choosing a subject along with different cases of basic construction methods up to cleaning and assembling resin parts and soldering photo etched brass. In the second book I cover the painting phases in equal detail using different examples. Applying basecoats to various paint chipping methods are demonstrated along with different examples and methods of

weathering. These books are not just about techniques such as soldering, applying washes or using the hairspray method but also about how to use them together to obtain authentic looking results. You will see in many cases throughout these books that techniques work best when combined with other techniques in order to finish a painting stage such as creating chipping effects for example. As a result many techniques will be demonstrated in various examples throughout different chapters.

Before we begin the construction examples covered in this first volume, I would like to take a few pages to write about how I got to where I am now as well as a few other areas within the scale modelling hobby that you will encounter. This could give insight to those who are interested in getting more involved with the scale modelling industry.

HOW I GOT TO HERE

ONE OF MY COLLEGE PROFESSORS ONCE SAID TO THE CLASS THAT YOU NEED TO FIND OUT WHAT IT IS THAT YOU ARE GOOD AT, PURSUE IT WITH ALL THAT YOU HAVE, AND NEVER LOOK BACK.

I was around twenty when I heard her say that and it took me another ten years or so to understand the validity of that statement. Although at times it is easier said than done, I have found that I have often remembered this phrase again and again practically over the past ten years.

I am now forty three years old and have been modelling since I was nine. How much I purchased and built models as a teenager, prior to the internet, depended upon the availability of kits in the department stores around my small town. I built them out of the box without painting or even taking the time to clean seams, fill gaps or sand away excess glue. After high school I ended up enrolling into a two-year program at a technical college to study the welding trade.

During the end of my first year I ended up traveling home one weekend to notice that a small store called AJ's Hobbyshop had opened up in my town. On an impulse I decided to stroll on in for a quick look around. The small shop was lit more from the front windows than from the few rows of florescent lights on the ceiling overhead. The air, lightly filled with lazily rolling patches of cigarette smoke, contained a mixed aroma of paint thinner, glue, cigarettes and coffee. Against the wall to my right was a set of shelves containing an impressive collection of assembled painted military models such as AFVs, trucks and planes from all eras. Many more planes of all scales where also strung from the ceiling. Most of the models already had a fine layer of dust. To my left was a workbench containing a cash register which I will talk about shortly. In the background I saw a semi-organized assortment of brand new fresh colorful model kits still in the plastic wrap. Also present were different racks of paints, after-market items of all sorts and magazines. Some of the brands I recognized from the department stores of my younger years but the others I had, until then, never even known existed, not to mention the after-market stuff. Best of all there was no RC stuff anywhere to be found.

Without even thinking I immediately walked down one of the rows to the shelves

containing the armour models, pulled a 1/35th scale Tamiya West German Leopard from the stack and brought it back towards the front of the shop, plopped it on the counter next to the register and impatiently started reaching into my pockets for my wallet. Al (AJ) Barden, the owner, who I would later refer to as the Lemmy Kilmister of modelling was a rather tall man in his fifties sporting a gray beard wearing old jeans and a faded denim shirt. He had a large dusty work bench behind the register stacked with opened boxes of kits, sprues, cut lengths of styrene sheets, glues, overhead lamps and various modelling tools. In the middle of these semi-organized piles was a small space. This space was like a small clearing in a huge jungle containing a partly completed military truck that he was scratch building along with various pliers, tweezers, an ashtray containing a lit cigarette and a stained chipped mug half full with coffee.

He broke his concentration from the project, slowly leaned back in his squeaky reclining office chair and lazily looked at me over his bifocals and asked me in a deep passive voice, "You like armour?" I really didn't care to make conversation with Al at the time because I was eager to get home and glue together my new kit. I just remember quickly saying yes, handing him a $20, collecting my change and quickly walking out the door with a new mission under my arm.

With Al (AJ) Barden 2014

That was in the spring of 1991. Over the months that followed I frequented AJ's Hobbyshop in a never ending quest for new kits, advice and industry news. There were always some guys from the local International Plastic Modellers' Society (IPMS) chapter hanging around sipping coffee at AJ's. I eventually became friends with Al, hanging out with him and the others on the weekends in his shop discussing the hobby while pawing though the latest modelling magazines and catalogues. At first I had absolutely no interest in painting the models I built as I was more concerned with just having something to glue together and man, did they look awful. Over the weeks my construction skills did improve and Al started trying to persuade me to paint them as well in which I had no interest. I think that it was the discouraged look that he finally gave me one day over his bifocals after asking me once again that persuaded me to finally give in and invest in some paint.

The following year I completed the two year welding program which I was enrolled in and started working full time as a welder/metal fabricator. I was working nights and building models during the day. Around that time I also, again from Al's advice, joined the local IPMS chapter, Southern Maine Scale Modellers (SMSM). The IPMS is made up of a bunch of local chapters and national branches of hobbyists interested in promoting and assembling plastic model kits. These chapters frequently organize annual meetings and visit events such as museums and vehicle exhibits. Joining SMSM got me attending the monthly meetings and yearly shows/competitions put on by the various IPMS chapters throughout New England. It was at these shows that I further learned about the basics regarding how to build and paint scale models. Winning awards came only with practice, time, always asking questions and persistence. Visiting these shows was when I was able to find some of the foreign magazines like Steel Masters (France) and Armour Modelling (Japan). It was in the pages of these publications that I first became familiar and influenced by Tony Greenland, Makoto Takaishi, Masahiro Doi and others. During one of these shows I found Tony Greenland's Panzer Modelling Master Class. I remember sitting at the restaurant Denny's until two in the morning reading that book all the way through and realizing that I wanted to someday make a similar publication myself.

The people in the SMSM club have been a strong source of friendship, encouragement, support and guidance. Today I credit Al Barden and the others who have been involved with SMSM over the years as the ones who got me started and have contributed in helping me to grow within this hobby. Today I am still a member of this organization attending the meeting on the first Tuesday of every month. Around 1998 a friend in SMSM asked me to

attend the national show by the Armour Modelling and Preservation Society (AMPS) in which I did rather well. By that time I had been attending the IPMS shows for a number of years and my work had improved. During this show I met Andrew Dextras, a young webmaster of a new internet page called Missing Lynx. Over the following months Andrew and his friend Nick Cortese persuaded me to get more involved with Missing Lynx contributing work for the gallery along with articles. The internet was still fairly new to me. I had visited other pages like Panzernet and Track-Link only to view the work. By that time I had decided to go back to school for a bachelor's degree. I was also working full time with a company designing lift tables for industrial and ergonomic applications.

Trying to balance a full-time profession, school and a desire to get more involved with the modelling industry was often difficult. I had only limited time for assembling and painting anything. Although complicated it was during those busy years that I started using the internet to obtain information about the hobby. The internet had become a never ending source for finding photos of work and articles by other modellers from around the world. The internet also made it much easier to locate kits and aftermarket accessories for upcoming projects. I also formed a network of people from a handful of different countries in which to obtain guidance, exchange information and discuss methods as well as ideas.

I eventually found some time to write my first article for Missing-Lynx and started submitting photos of my work for the gallery

there. I had by then been talking daily with some of the Spanish modellers like Miguel Jimenez, Luciano and Alvaro Rodriguez and a number of others. These people gave me much help with the current finishing theories along with the photography skills needed for publishing my work.

During the summer of 2001, I traveled to Barcelona, Spain for a week to visit Miguel Jimenez. Luciano was also there. It is still one of the most memorable weeks of my life. I was very impressed with how modern Barcelona was and I immediately knew that Europe was the next step for me. During that week with Miguel I learned a lot of the basics of working with different mediums such as pigments, acrylics, enamel and oil paints along with when to effectively use them together. Knowing how to use these mediums collectively is very important as you will see in numerous examples throughout the second book.

The following year I was invited to visit Japan for two weeks with Miguel and Luciano. Japan was a cultural experience for me like no other since. It took me a few days to get habituated to the customs. Japan was only the second foreign country that I had visited at the time. During my stay we were able to visit a number of museums and other well-known historical locations. We also got to see the renowned hobby store Yellow Submarine and visit Artbox, the publishers of Armour Modelling and Model Graphics magazines.

Having drinks in Tokyo the famous Japanese modeller and a personal influence of mine Masahiro Doi.

Toward the end of the trip we attended the famous Shizuoka Modelling show. Shizuoka is an exposition and not a contest. Therefore, there were no rules giving the hobbyists who attended much more creative freedom to express their imagination in the models they exhibit. I have never seen anything like Shizuoka since.

While in Japan my first article was printed in England with, at the time, a new magazine called AFV Modeller. The article went over well and it helped me to develop a good rapport with the editors that I still have today. The exposure given to my articles by AFV Modeller has played a big role in helping me to get noticed and published in the magazines and books with other publishers in countries such as Italy, Spain, Germany, Japan, Hungary, Poland, Holland and now the US.

In 2005 I moved to Spain to work for Mig Productions. I was employed there for five years.

Inside MIG Productions 2006

During that time I gained experience with creating, mixing, sourcing and producing new products. I also established contacts and relationships with people on the business side of the scale modelling industry. The environment during the first years inside Mig Productions also allowed me to finish some of my most successful projects up to that time. I was able to obtain further knowledge about painting when finishing company models for the box art of products such as the civilian finishes on the Hi-Lux and other technical's including the BJ44 and 45s. I was single so I would go into work for eight hours than spend another four hours or so in the evenings building and painting my own subjects such as the Red Krupp Ardelt and Panther F which were my first attempts in experimenting with what would later become known as the Colour Modulation Style.

This Toyoda Hi-Lux was a company project for MIG Productions. It was my first work on a model containing a civilian finish. The finish was a joint effort done by Andres Montiel, Miguel Jimenez and myself.

This Krupp was my first attempt at experimenting with what would become the Color Modulation Style.

During the Mig Productions years I also started traveling abroad to different shows giving seminars. These trips helped to promote both Mig Productions and myself as I established more contacts along the way. I would visit shows in three, four and even five different countries during a year. Some of the people that I met during these times have since become very good friends who have helped me tremendously such as with these books for example and with my new company WILDER.

Almost five years to the day I ended up leaving Mig Productions. Management had changed and I felt that I had gone as far as I was going to go there. It was one of the most difficult decisions of my life. I was invited by a good friend Harry Steinmüller to stay in Southern Germany for a few months so I flew from Spain straight to Germany. Like Spain, I also found that I really enjoyed living in rural Bavaria. During these months I spent a lot of time walking the Bavarian countryside deciding what I was going to do next. My stay was cut a bit short when a close relative/good friend became very ill.

After being back in the states for a few months I ended up flying over to Moscow Russia to start my own company WILDER. I had met the people whom I'm working with now when I visited the year prior to give a series of seminars on modelling. The people involved with WILDER in Moscow created a different environment. They have been very open, professional, creative and practical. I think that living under communism and the economical problems that followed during Perestroika has made the Russians accustomed to getting by with less, making them more resourceful. Moscow and the other cities in Russia that I have visited today have all of the amenities of the west but the resourcefulness of the people around me is still present.

Russia has its own culture. It took me a bit longer to get comfortable with living there then when I was in Spain. For a while I was considering the possibility of staying in Moscow but decided to come home after four years to be closer to my family. The people working with me in Russia have given me a much new insight on both business and art which has allowed me to build further upon what I learned both in Spain and before. Today most of my modelling efforts are directed toward my new company WILDER.

These two books are a project that I have been putting together between others for the past eight years. They contain just about everything I have both learned and taught myself about constructing and painting armour models starting with AJ's Hobby Shop back in 1991, up though Moscow, Russia today. The construction methods and techniques that I will cover are largely a result of the American IPMS and AMPS shows that taught me the importance of the

AMT Torrent 2009 with Mario Eens, Alessandro Bruschi and Wim Van Hool

fundamentals for the technical side of scale modelling seen in the first book. It was living, working and traveling though out Europe that gave me much of the artistic knowledge that has helped me to both learn and create the different finishing methods covered in the second book.

It's nothing new when I say that someone needs to be extremely devoted and work very hard in order to advance and be successful in any type of profession. Part of the reason that I have gotten to where I am during the finishing of

these two books is also because of a lot of unique opportunities, a love for the hobby, a desire to be creative and a supportive group of family and friends who have helped to guide me. I ended up finding something that I was good at, pursued it and (for the most part) I haven't looked back. Let's now continue by quickly talking about what is available to armour modellers today such as what's on the market and a few of the social aspects.

After a presentation in Moscow Russia 2010

WHAT'S AVAILABLE TO MODELLERS TODAY

MANY MODELLERS HAVE REFERRED TO THE PAST TEN YEARS OR SO AS "THE GOLDEN AGE" OF ARMOUR MODELLING.

This is because almost every subject that we can think of is available in rather affordable injection moulded kits. In the recent years many new manufacturers have appeared on the market with frequent releases of even the oddest vehicles. Some companies appear to concentrate much of their efforts on "Paper Panzers" which only existed as a quick sketch according to the wildest fantasies of German engineers during WWII. These subjects were only available to us in the past as expensive resin kits, often of poor quality, that took much experience and patience to assemble and paint. The more common subjects such as the German Tiger I are available in different scales at various qualities in a wide price range.
There are also endless numbers of upgrade sets

such as single link tracks, resin accessories, photo etched bass sets, metal barrels and so on. For those who are willing to buy all the extra detail sets a single model can easily cost upwards of around 200€ and more. But then again the standard of today's injection moulded plastic kits is so high that they can be built out of the box and many feel that there is no real need to put too much effort into extra detailing. Nowadays many kits even include metal barrels and photo etched details at a reasonable price.
The finishing products also play a big role today.

Various companies offer all kinds of pigments, washes and oil paints, especially designed for the needs of armour modellers to finish their models quicker. Many of these products are developed for a specific subject or purpose, making it rather easy to obtain satisfying results during the weathering stage.

With friends viewing one of the few remaining King Tiger tanks on display in La Gleize Belgium during 2010.

HOW MUCH WOULD YOU LIKE TO GET INVOLVED WITH THIS HOBBY?

BY DEFINITION, A HOBBY IS SOMETHING THAT WE DO IN OUR FREE TIME TO HAVE FUN AND FOR RELAXATION.

For the vast majority of us this is the case for sure. Nothing is better than relaxing after work or school while assembling a model of the tank you saw in that World War II documentary last week. But for some it may become more than that over time. There are modelling forums and clubs that can help to provide you with a lot of pointers and information to improve. But with clubs and forums often come contests and shows that need to be organized. It really depends upon how involved you would like to get. You might want to ask yourself why you chose armour modelling as a hobby and what are your goals with it. Is it fun and relaxation? Is it also for historical or social interest? Over time many of us will choose to build models to attend shows and contests. Shows and contests will certainly encourage you to improve. As you improve you may even be asked to build models to publish in magazines or even for collectors. All of this can be rather rewarding allowing you to also make a bit of extra money on the side.

Just remember that if you get to a point where you are trying to earn money with your

A photo of an exhibit table at the Scale Model Challenge show in Eindhoven Netherlands during the 2012 show.

modelling it will not be as enjoyable anymore. Sometimes you will have to deal with deadlines. Nothing takes the fun out of scale modelling like a deadline. You need to try to avoid them when possible if you are publishing but that will not always be the case. Professional modelling brings pressure along with it. You certainly loose a bit of creative freedom when an editor tells you what to build next or if you are doing commission work. Most modellers enjoy a bit of a trade off but the more involved you get the less fun you will have. If you do not plan carefully and time becomes

too limited you will notice that the quality of your work will diminish under these circumstances. Being involved with the modelling industry at even a semi-professional level might appear more attractive than it actually is. Therefore how much you choose to get involved is up to you. I recommend that if asked to publish articles or do commissions you first consider the size of the project, how much time you have at your disposal and if the end result will be worth your time or not. Saying "no" upfront is better than not being able to follow though.

INVOLVEMENT WITH FORUMS AND FACEBOOK

THE INTERNET HAS HAD A HUGE IMPACT ON THE HOBBY AS A WHOLE. KITS AND REFERENCE MATERIAL ARE MUCH EASIER TO ACCESS THAN THEY WERE 15 YEARS AGO.

You can also obtain inspiration by seeing the work posted by other modellers and you can upload your own models to get feedback on your efforts. Forums are great for this purpose but can be a double edged sword. Some are presenting their work to get constructive criticism in order to improve their skills which is great. But other times critical remarks have been given on forums causing disputes more than once. There are many forums out there with different groups of people frequenting them. It is not uncommon that it may take someone a few tries before finding a forum with a group of individuals where they feel comfortable spending their time discussing the hobby. When you decide to post your work in a forum you should be aware of the following. You can get responses you won't like to read because they are either negative or maybe even too positive. You could get very little or even no response which might mean that people do not care for the model too much. Make yourself clear. Ask the community to point out what they like and dislike about the model. Try to be as informative as possible in your description and introduction of the posted model. The more information that you provide to the visitors on the forum the better they can judge your efforts. Social media now also plays an important role with the scale modelling hobby. Recently Facebook has taken some attention from the Forums. Here you can actually chose your "friends" but if you look at the numbers of friends people actually have listed in their profiles, Facebook now appears to be the biggest forum of them all. The modelling industry is also taking advantage of this form of networking. Nowadays Facebook is heavily used for product placement measures and announcements for new releases which can be quite informative when not overdone. Forums and social networks are great for getting in touch with likeminded people from all over the world.

MODEL CLUBS AND CHAPTERS

PRIOR TO THE INTERNET ERA, CLUB MEETINGS AND SHOWS WERE THE BIGGEST SOURCE FOR MODELLERS TO EXCHANGE THEIR THOUGHTS AND IDEAS.

Despite the fact that there are countless modelling related online communities, the club meetings are still very popular. They add a social aspect to an otherwise very individual hobby and a chance to make new friends. You often can't compare seeing a picture of a model on the internet with actually viewing it for real. Attending club meetings is also very helpful when you are trying to improve your skills. Other members give advice to novices, helping them to improve. There are some chapters and clubs with a worldwide reputation. Both IPMS and AMPS are international chapters that have been around for years. An example of a good club is the Kempense Modellbouw Club (KMK) from Belgium. Their annual show attracts modellers from all over the world.

Enjoying a ride on one of my favorite AFVs in Finland.

Armoured vehicle demonstration at the 5th FMSS Military Land Vehicle Model Competition.

SHOWS AND COMPETING

FOR THOSE WHO CANNOT ATTEND CLUB MEETINGS, MODEL SHOWS ARE A GREAT OPPORTUNITY FOR MEETING LIKEMINDED PEOPLE AND VIEWING THE WORK OF OTHERS.

Most shows have a large number of vendors present and for many attendees these weekends sometimes turn out to be just as expensive as they are fun. There are also sometimes demonstrations from well known modellers showing their techniques and approaches to the audience. Seeing these people actually perform the techniques is a great way to learn new skills.

Most shows also host competitions. One of the world's most reputable shows/competitions is arguably Euromilitaire in Folkestone, England. Originally being a figure show, it nowadays attracts some of the best armour modellers from all over the world. The work displayed on the tables is always very inspirational. AMT Torrent near Valencia, Spain, is another very impressive show with an extremely nice venue.

When it comes to competitions happiness and frustration often come hand and hand like at any other type of competition. While it can be very satisfying when a model gets an award it can also be disappointing when one does not achieve what they were hoping for. The judging systems vary from show to show but the results always come down to the opinion of a rather small group of people. You have to keep in mind that judging a model is a very subjective thing. There are no goals, inches or seconds to count to find out who wins. It's only the question if a few judges like the subject, the style of finish it contains and the weathering for example. We should all try to keep in mind that modelling is not about competing. If that is the case you will find yourself possibly getting frustrated from time to time. Keeping all this in mind lets now start getting into constructing armour models and why assembly is so important.

A combined seminar with friend and renowned Russian modeller Vladimir Yashin at the DiSH Modelling Event in Moscow city 2012.

Presentation hall at the Nordic Challenge Scale Modelling Exhibition in Finland 2013

BEFORE WE START, WHY ASSEMBLY IS SO IMPORTANT

OVER THE PAST YEARS AS A RESULT OF THE AVAILABILITY OF HIGH QUALITY KITS COVERING A BROAD SPECTRUM OF SUBJECTS, NEW FINISHING METHODS AND STYLES ALONG WITH AN ATTEMPT BY COMPANIES TO SELL MORE PAINTING AND WEATHERING PRODUCTS, THE DETAILING OF KITS ALONG WITH SCRATCH-BUILDING HAS BECOME LESS COMMON.

If you are creative, just as much imagination can be incorporated into the build which will only serve to further enhance the finish. One example that you will see throughout these two books is this German Tiger I. The flaked zimmerit, damaged wheels, bent fenders and impacts were all enough to show any viewer that this unpainted model was going to be a veteran Tiger containing heavy weathering. When finished, all of those rather easy construction characteristics work together with the muddied winter camouflage, heavy coats of mud and wet effects to create an authentic looking Tiger tank struggling against a numerically superior Soviet army in the difficult winter conditions of the Eastern Front. A good creative build can also completely change the look of a common subject like this theoretical Soviet IS-3 in the battle of Berlin also seen though out both of the books. Therefore the construction methods discussed in this first book are just as important as the painting methods covered in the next one.

Don't forget that knowing the basics, such as properly cleaning seams and filling pin marks will allow you to build more authentic models while also competing better at the shows. After the gallery we will continue on page 76 with discussing some important fundamental techniques on assembling models. These basic methods will be covered up to assembling plastic tracks on page 109. After that we move on to more involved construction techniques and mediums.

GALLERY MODELS

38TX WALKER:

Resin Mig Productions kit designed by Michael Fichtenmayer. Chipped using the traditional sponge and brush method. Weathered using Tamiya paints, pigments and brown enamels mixed with a bit of enamel gloss.

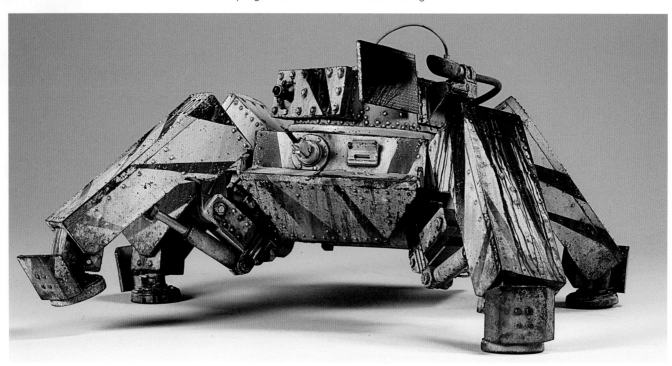

GERMAN 30,5CM SFL BÄR PAPER PANZER:

This subject was the focus of a seven-part series of scratch-building articles which appeared in 'Art of Modelling' magazine during 2013 and 2014. The replica was built from Evergreen sheet plastic using parts and overall dimensions taken from the full resin kit by New Connection Models. Other bits such as the hatches and running gear were cut from the DML Models Porsche Jagdtiger kit. Aber photo etch and Friulmodel tracks were also employed. This self-propelled gun was probably protecting some German occupied port as a result of the Kriegsmarine type camouflage. Figure painted by Ivan Cocker.

GERMAN GESCHÜTZWAGEN TIGER FUR 17CM KANONE 72 (SF):

This model was the main subject of a DVD that I worked on with MXpression entitled, "Authentic Metal". The model is the Trumpeter kit built mostly from the box. Most of the weld seams needed to be added. Parts from a Voyager photo etch kit were also used along with Friulmodel tracks. Figure by Ivan Cocker.

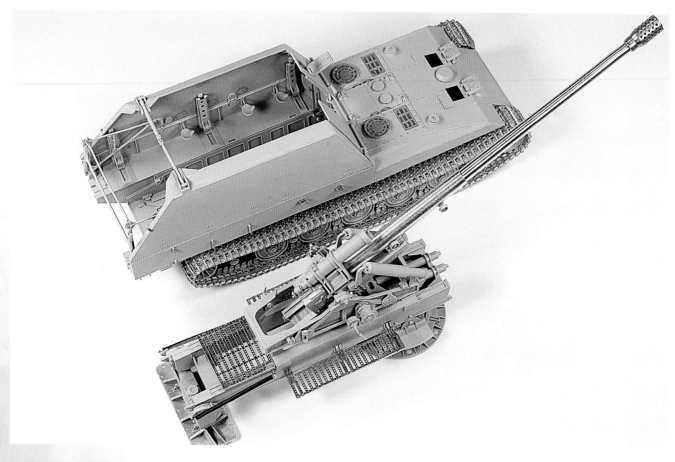

GERMAN E-50 PAPER PANZER:

This theoretical subject was painted to look like it was containing only a coat of red oxide primer. The steel surfaces were a result of viewing numerous scrap metal photos and attempting to duplicate the colors and textures observed. The Trumpeter E-50 kit was used. Aber photo etch and parts scratch-built from copper sheet. Tracks from Friulmodel. Figures by Ivan Cocker.

GERMAN E-75 PAPER PANZER:

It's great that companies like Trumpeter have now made these Paper Panzers available to us at reasonable prices. The problem is that some work is required to improve them such as with the E-75 and E-50 kits for example. In this case I rescribed and added all of the weld seams on the hull to obtain the proper scaled thicknesses of the plates. The 10.5cm/L68 KwK gun is from Zitader. Aber photo etch and Friulmodel tracks were employed. The Turm-Winkel Zielfernrohr 3 stabilized periscopic gun sight was also scratched using evergreen.

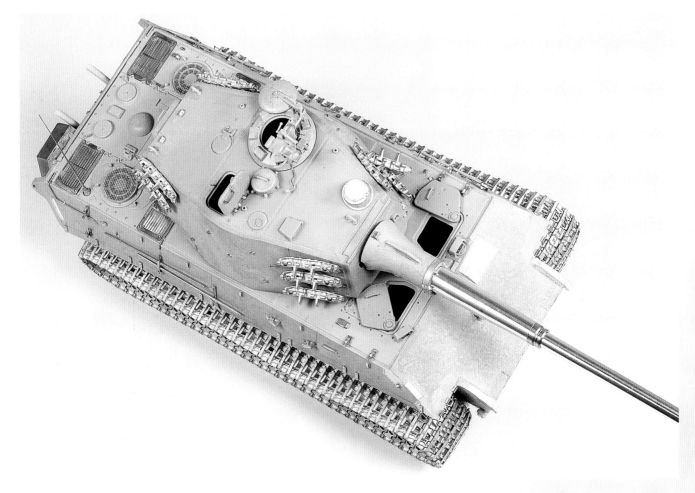

CZECH HETZER, PRAGUE 1945:

Based on actual photos, this Hetzer like the E-50 was a way for me to challenge myself while trying to duplicate what I saw in a collection of various steel images I had found online. Eduard model, photo etch and Friulmodel tracks.

GERMAN JADGTIGER: The focus of the Colour Modulation DVD from Mig Productions released in 2008. DML kit with Aber Photo etch and Friulmodel tracks. Photos by Miguel Jimenez

GERMAN JAGDPANTHER NO. 112, SCHWERE PANZERJAGER ABTEILUNG 654.:

Containing all Friulmodel metal tracks, this is probably the heaviest model I ever finished. Model constructed by Jorge Alvear. Tamiya kit with Aber photo etch and resin zimmerit.

SOVIET JS-3 M45:

Hypothetical subjects such as this IS-3 are very enjoyable. When chosen carefully they allow you to pitch your own spin on popular commonly modelled subjects such as this one. The Tamiya kit was used along with photo etch from Aber and ET-Model. The mattress and spaced armour was scratch-built using copper sheet and brass screening. Friulmodel tracks were also used.

SOVIET OBJECT 701 NO 5, 1944 PROTOTYPE, BATTLE FOR MAINLAND JAPAN:

This is the Trumpeter JS-4 kit backdated to an Object 701 No 5, 1944 Prototype. Aber photo etch was used along with other bits built from evergreen plastic and copper sheet. Friulmodel wheels have also been added. I painted a chipped camouflage over the model in layers using the hairspray technique. Although the colors are a bit different this type of scheme represents some of the camouflages seen on Soviet Tanks during the Cold War. Figures painted by Ivan Cocker. Weathered using WILDER products.

SOVIET JSU-152:

Tamiya kit built from the box. Only the lights were wired. Damage to the fenders was created using pliers, a razor saw and hobby knife.

GERMAN KRUPPSTEYR WAFFENTRAGER PROTOTYPE:

This subject is one of my older projects built back in 2006. It was my first experiments with what would eventually become the Colour Modulation Style. Full resin kit from New Connection Models.

GERMAN KRUPP/ARDELT WAFFENTRAGER 88MM PAK-43:

Trumpeter kit with Aber photo etch and Friulmodel tracks. Fenders scratch-built from copper sheet.

KV-2X WALKER:

Resin Mig Productions kit designed by Michael Fichtenmayer. This project was one of the first experimentations with the hairspray method covered in the second book. Note how the wet effects help to add more texture to the big blocky matt rusty turret which might have been rather plain otherwise.

SOVIET KV-1 M42:

Trumpeter kit with Aber photo etch and Friulmodel tracks. Weathered using WILDER products. Painted using the New Color Modulation Style.

A series of videos are available about weathering this model on YouTube at: www.YouTube.com/WILDER.

U.S. LVT-(A) 1, SAIPAN 1944:

Revel Kit constructed by Daryl Dancik mostly built from the box updated with a few Verlinden bits and Friulmodel tracks. I chose this subject for its weathering potential. The thick layers of wet mud were made from built up layers of pigments and fixer. Vallejo Still Water was used to obtain the glossy wet appearance over these muddy areas. Figure painted by Ivan Cocker. Painted using the New Color Modulation Style.

U.S. M113A1, VIETNAM:

The old Academy kit with Eduard photo etch and Friulmodel tracks. Bravo-6 figures painted by Ivan Cocker. From the beginning of its assembly I knew that this project would need to be about the figures as I always found static M113A1s to be rather simple in shape. Weathered using WILDER products.

U.S. M4 SHERMAN, OKANAWA 1945:

Dragon kit from the box with MIG Production resin/PE conversion set.

GERMAN PANTHER F:

This model was important for my career for a couple of reasons. I had finally obtained a true feel for what would become the Colour Modulation style. It was also the first model where I started to rely on speckling as a means for enhancing both chipping and weathering effects. Cyber Hobby kit with Aber photo etched brass and copper sheet details, Friulmodel tracks and scratch-built stand-off roof armour.

GERMAN PANZER IV H
4TH PANZER-DIVISION:

Another one of my older builds and a personal favorite. I used this model to see how far I could take the colour modulation style. The hull and turret schuetzens made it perfect for applying deep shadows and highlights. Tamiya kit with Aber photo etch and Friulmodel tracks. Figure painted by César Oliva.

SOVIET T-34/85:

A more recent subject that I had wanted to build for years. The German Thoma shields gave this famous AFV such a unique appearance. This model was used as the focus of a DVD released by WILDER entitled, "Dealing with Photoetch". DML kit with Aber photo etch, Friulmodel tracks and converted Tamyia Panther G road wheels were used. Resin turret manufacturer unknown.

SOVIET T-34/122:

Another theoretical subject weathered with WILDER products. Figure painted by Ivan Cocker.

DML T-34 kit with Aber photo etch and Friulmodel tracks. Resin turret available from WILDER.

T-62 SCRAP HULL, AFGHANISTAN:

Although I initially thought the opposite, I found it to be more time consuming and tedious when painting a subject while referencing clear colour photos. Model constructed by Zackary Vincent

Sex. Figure painted by Ivan Cocker. Trumpeter T-62 with Voyager photo etch.
Weathered using WILDER products.

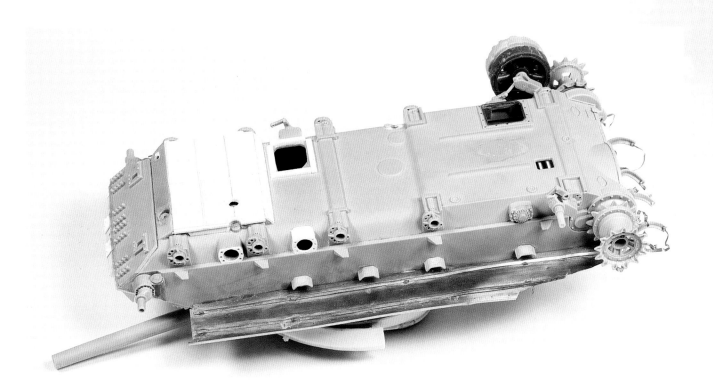

GERMAN TIGER I, FALL 1943 PRODUCTION:

This model was a converted to a fall of 1943 production type by combining two kits. The two models used were the Dragon Pz.Kpfw.VI Ausf.E Sd.Kfz.181 Tiger 1 Late Production and the Cyber Hobby Dragon Tiger I DAK Initial Production Tunisia. Aber photo each and Friulmodel tracks were also needed. The zimmerit around the turret was created using two-part Apoxie Sculpt while on the hull Morimori putty was used. Figures painted by Calvin Tan.

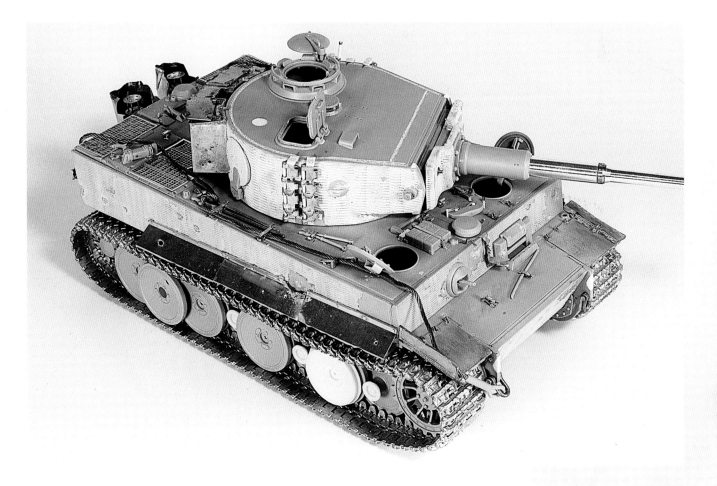

TRES TRISTES TIGRES:

This project was completed in colaberation with the MIG Productions staff. Figure by Miguel Jimenez. Francois Verdier and Miguel Jimenez also aided with the base and groundwork. Photos by Miguel Jimenez..

GERMAN VK3001:

Trumpeter kit built pretty much from the box. Scratch built rear rack and spare track mounts.

ModelKasten track links.

HERE WE GO.
IN THIS CHAPTER WE ARE GOING TO COVER THE COMMON SKILLS NEEDED TO ASSEMBLE A GOOD MODEL.

Some points will be a review for many while others are more advanced. All of them are important. If you can obtain a decent understanding of the basic techniques and an ability to adequately perform them than you are well on your way. Choosing subjects to construct is very important. There are a number of factors to consider when doing so. First of all I would always recommend starting with the vehicles that interest you the most. I would also suggest closed top AFVs because they are easier to both assemble and paint. Using presumably good kits from reputable manufactures will also save you a bit of time and frustration. Not all kits produced by respectable model companies are so expensive such as the new kits from Trumpeter for example. The pointers above are probably some of the reasons why the King Tiger, T-34 and Sherman tanks are always so popular with modellers. They are well documented and rather simple closed topped vehicles containing a lot of history. These subjects are also easily available in kits of good quality.

When I got started I built mostly T-34s and KV tanks from the box with only basic detailing for years. I was an American in collage with a part time job and I simply found these Russian subjects to be historical, exotic and most importantly quick to assemble.

Having built these rather easy subjects helped me to master the basic but most important assembly and painting practices needed to generate conversation when displaying my work at the local IPMS shows and club meetings.

During those days the internet was only in its infancy. Either at a meeting or on the web, it is much easier when you are just starting out, to discuss a few problems at a time on decent manufactured models than to do so about the numerous flaws often encountered on poorly designed kits. Discussing both your work and the efforts of others is the greatest way to exchange ideas, knowledge and techniques helping you to improve while obtaining further motivation at the same time. You will also make new acquaintances and friends which is one of the most rewording parts of any hobby.

CRITICAL ASSEMBLY FUNDAMENTALS

THE SU-152 KIT MANUFACTURED BY TAMIYA IS RELATIVELY NEW. IT IS FAIRLY ACCURATE AND ASSEMBLES NICELY.

It is also well documented while also containing that imposing Soviet look making it popular amongst armour modellers. This JSU-152 will be put together covering most of the basic assembly practices. During this part we will be going over topics such as filling pin marks,

quickly and effectively gluing parts along with basic texturing. Wiring headlights and assembling track will also be covered. Let's get started with the most basic but important practice of cleaning seams.

CUTTING, CLEANING AND SANDING PARTS

IN THE FOLLOWING SEGMENT I AM GOING TO SHOW YOU THE TECHNIQUES AND TOOLS THAT I USE TO CUT, CLEAN AND PREPARE PLASTIC MODEL PARTS FOR ASSEMBLY.

To start, sprues are what the parts in a kit come attached to. They are like a frame to hold the parts. Seams and pin marks are left over on the parts from the injection molding process used to manufacture the sprues. We will discuss how to eliminate pin marks later. The seams are a result of where the two parts of the molds are pressed together. In some of the older low-end kits the seams are very prominent due to bad alignment of the moulds. So bad that after the parts are cleaned you are left with deformed grab handles and gun barrels for example. Many manufacturers of the kits on the market today have severely minimized the seams present on their sprues but we still need to deal with them. Cleaning parts sounds easy but it is a small art form within itself which takes practice. Veteran modellers who have cleaned so many parts over the years do so with grace and finesse without even realizing it. Seams, bits of the sprue and pin marks are the first thing that modellers will see when viewing your work. Here I will show you some of the tools and techniques I use to remove these annoying bits of plastic.

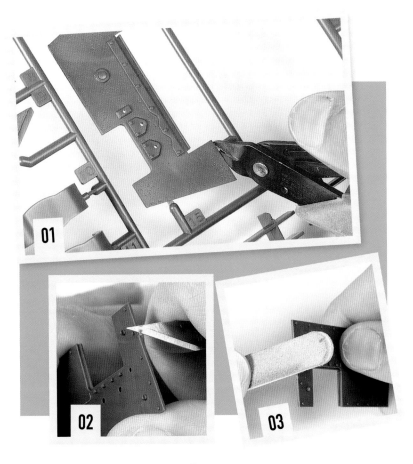

PHOTO 1 THROUGH 3:
You will first need to cut the parts from the sprue. I have seen people use wire cutters for this task but I strongly recommend side cutters made specifically for plastic. They allow for cleaner cuts closer to the parts. Most hobby stores offer various brands. Just ask the owners of your local hobby store or search for them on-line.

After removing the part use a sharp hobby knife to whittle away any of the remaining bits of the sprue. Sharp number 11 blades work the best for this task. Use a file or sanding stick to finish cleaning the areas that were whittled clean.

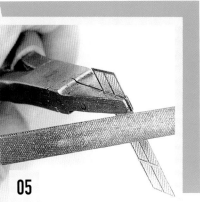

PHOTO 4 AND 5: :
Photo etched parts are included with most kits today. You will need to cut these parts in the same manner and clean them using a file.

PHOTO 6 THROUGH 8:
Sometimes parts can be complex and regular plastic cutters might damage the detail. Sharp hobby blades are one way to get around this problem. Blades come in an array of shapes and sizes that can be used for cleaning and cutting parts to remove unwanted bits of plastic. In time you will develop your own preference for the blades to use during various tasks.

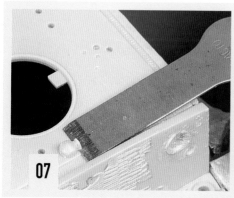

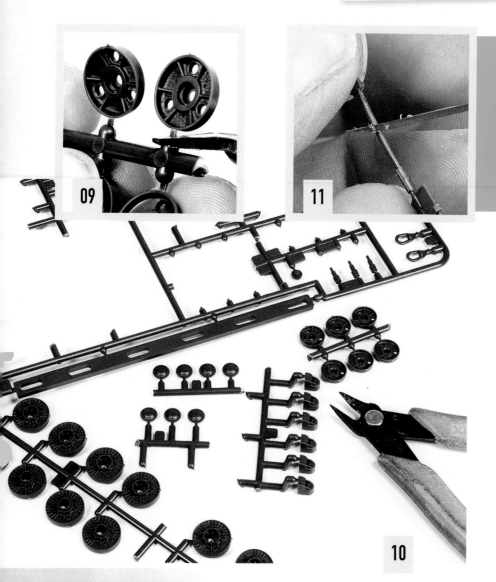

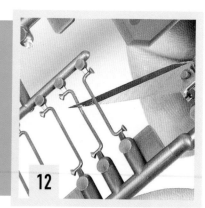

PHOTO 9 AND 10:
You may want to sometimes cut the smaller parts away from the sprues in sections such as the components which make up the running gear. Doing so will make it easier to carefully cut away the rest of the unneeded plastic close to the pieces minimizing cleanup.

PHOTO 11 AND 12:
After cutting the parts you can remove the seams in a number of ways. The most common method is with the back of your hobby knife. Today as modelling kits become more advanced we are required to clean finer more fragile plastic parts. I would recommend cleaning as much of the seams from fragile parts prior to removing them from the sprue. You can use the sprue as a handle while carefully cleaning the part.

PHOTO 13 AND 14:

Sanding sheets and files are also important for cleaning fine parts. With sandpaper you will want to have a number of different grits on hand. The grit refers to the number of particles per square inch or centimeter. The higher the grit the smoother the sandpaper. Sanding sheets can be purchased in a hobby store. You can also buy inexpensive sheets of sanding paper in any hardware store. They usually come in sets containing all of the grits you will need from rough cleaning to fine polishing.

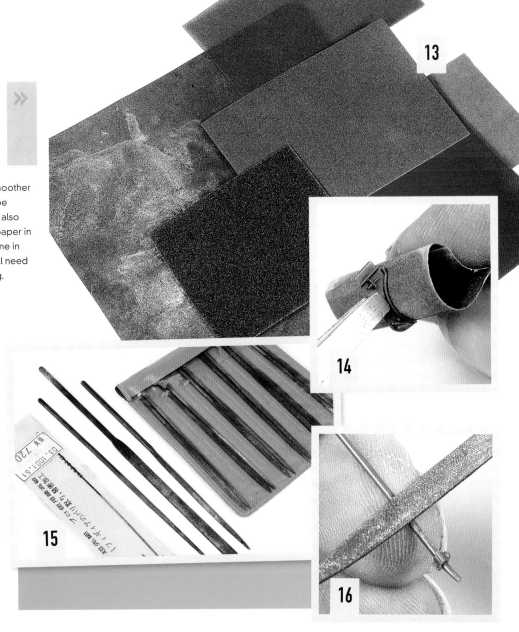

PHOTO 15 AND 16:

Files are available in a number of shapes and sizes. They are inexpensive and can be purchased in sets or separately. Fine metallic files are ideal for cleaning seams from fine detailed parts. I would recommend just getting a set that will give all of the shapes you will need for most applications. You will see different examples of how to use various files throughout this book.

PHOTO 17 AND 19:

Sanding sticks and blocks are also handy. The grits and shapes available are endless. I use sanding sticks mostly for cleaning the seams from larger simpler parts such as wheels. Sometimes you will get little burrs of plastic after you sand large parts. Lightly scrape the knife over the edge to deburr the part.

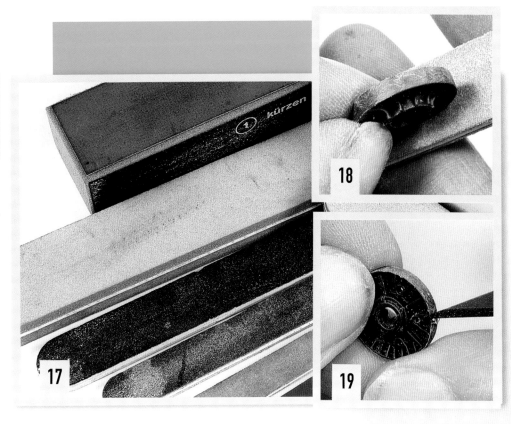

PHOTO 20 THROUGH 23:
This rigid flat sander is another very important tool to have in your arsenal. You can use it to quickly clean seams and remaining bits of the sprue where they are easily accessible. It is always best to go back over the cleaned parts after with lighter grit sanding sticks or films

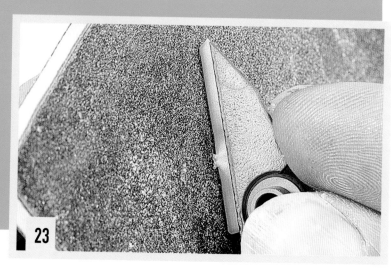

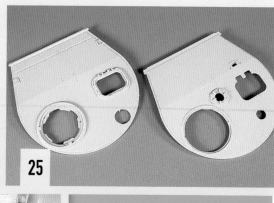

PHOTO 24 THROUGH 26:
A flat sander also can help with a number of other tasks. Here are a few examples. I needed to back date the turret on this Tiger I. After cutting the loaders hatch from the part I sanded the unwanted plastic away using a circular motion until only the details where left allowing me to glue it flush onto its new turret.

PHOTO 27 THROUGH 29:

I also use this tool to help me obtain symmetrical details as seen with these bits of plastic used to build up the front of the turret. I needed to super glue small strips onto each side of the roof in order to backdate it. Once the strips were firmly attached I sanded and shaped both sides at once as shown on photo 28.

These are just some examples of how I cut clean and sand parts. As you can see there are plenty of tools available to aid you in this task. More tools for these tasks will be shown in the next part of this book so let's continue with pin marks. pin marks are another nuisance that modellers need to deal with just like seams. Here are some methods that I often employ to fill and remove them.

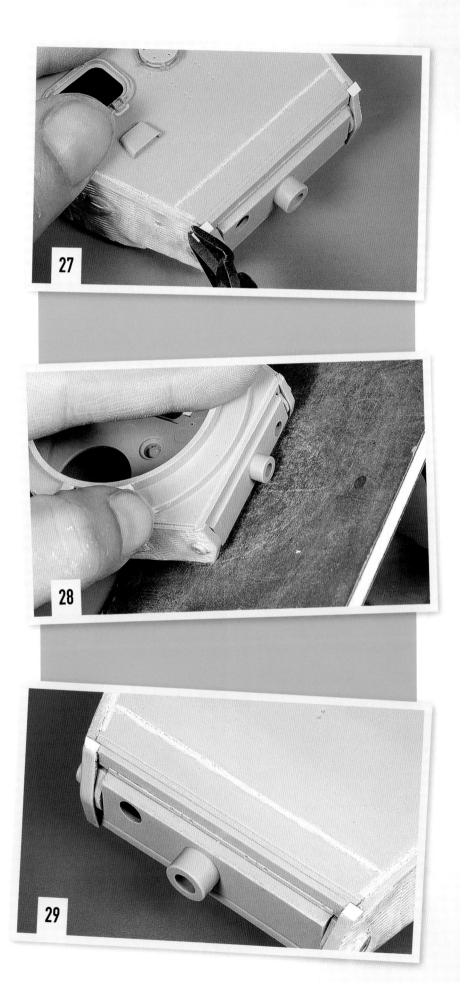

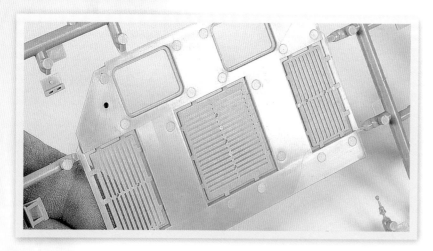

FILLING PIN MARKS & UNWANTED GAPS

PIN MARKS ARE SMALL CIRCULAR AREAS ON THE PARTS LEFT WHERE THE PLASTIC IS PUSHED OUT OF THE MOULDS.

Like seams, these circular areas are not on the actual vehicles and therefore inaccurate. Some pin marks are rather deep and must be filled with putty or super glue. Others can simply be sanded away.

Most of the pin marks in today's kits are carfully located by the manufacturers in places where they will not be visible on the assembled model.

This saves a bit of assembly time for the modeller, but conveniently locating pin marks where they will be unnoticed is not always so easy on complicated parts or pieces containing detail on both surfaces for example.

Another topic that I would like to discus in this chapter is unwanted gaps. Scale models are made up of many parts. Sometimes parts need to be moulded in two half's due to their complexity. Some examples of these pieces are large diameter gun barrels and cylindrical fuel tanks. After gluing these halves together you will have an unneeded gap. Gaps can also be a result of poorly designed and manufactured kits. This segment is to discuss techniques that will allow you to quickly fill these little flaws.

01

02

PHOTO 1 AND 2:
Putty is the most common medium used by modellers to fill pin marks. There are many types available on the market. I prefer Tamiya putty because it's soft and dries rather fast. After it has solidified you can carefully sand it smooth using sand paper. Start with heavier grades of sandpaper and finish using lighter ones.

04

05

06

PHOTO 4 THROUGH 6:
Using putty is also a great way to fill seams on textured surfaces. On my JSU I had a gap where the upper and lower part of the chassis mated together. After the two parts were firmly glued I placed a large amount of putty over the gap, let it dry for a few minutes, then textured it using a tapping motion with an old brush dampened with liquid cement.

03

PHOTO 3:
You can thin some types of putty using liquid cement or acetone to fill very fine pin marks as on the interior of this hatch.
The problem is that Tamiya putty tends to shrink a bit leaving a concave surface on deeper marks and gaps that will be noticeable through the basecoat when you paint the model. Therefore you may need to fill the hole, sand it smooth, then repeat the process a few more times.

07

«

PHOTO 7:
Using polyester putty is another method for filling unwanted holes and gaps. The brands that I have used are a bit thicker than the putties designed for plastic models so I tend to not use it on fine seams. The polyester putty will dry quickly and can be sanded within about five minutes. In fact, you need to apply it rather quickly.

08

PHOTO 8 THROUGH 11:
I needed to fill a number of holes intended for the placement of details on this Tiger I hull. Most of these details were replaced with photo etched parts. Just deposit some of the polyester putty onto a piece of plastic. Next, mix it thoroughly with a small amount of hardener using a toothpick. I quickly filled the holes with the putty then sanded them smooth all within about ten minutes. Remember to start with heaver grades of sandpaper and finish with lighter types insuring a smooth polished finish.

»

09

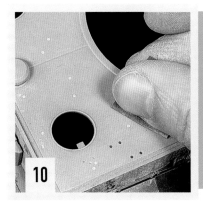

10

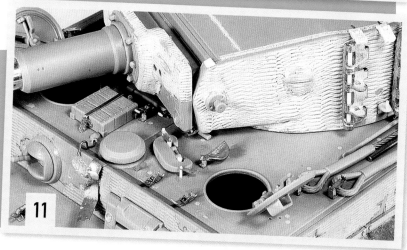

11

«

PHOTO 12 THROUGH 14:
Superglue and accelerator can be another quick, clean method for filling gaps. Accelerator can be purchased in most hobby stores. In the case of this rather large JSU-152 gun I carefully

aligned the two halves and applied liquid cement along the entire length of each seam on both sides. I let the glue dry for about 20 minutes.

It is convenient to know that superglue will

remain a liquid for almost an hour when placed into an aluminum bowl like in the photos. Apply the superglue along the entire seam. Next quickly apply accelerator over the super glue rapidly solidifying it. The dried super glue will form a rough convex contour.

12

13

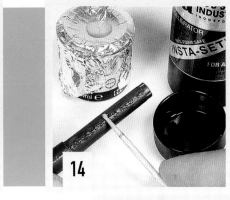

14

PHOTO 15 THROUGH 17:
A rough sanding stick was used to quickly remove the majority of the hard super glue. I finished sanding the barrel using a Flex file to help ensure that I did not sand away the outer diameter resulting in an oval shaped barrel. Flex files are great for cleaning circular objects.

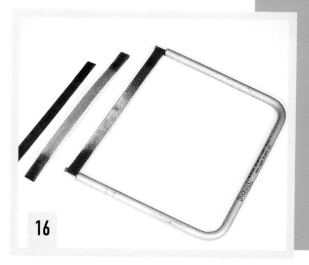

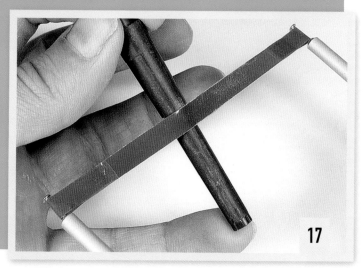

PHOTO 18 THROUGH 20:
Steel wool can be used to further polish plastic areas after they have been sanded smooth. I waited until the gap was filled and cleaned before gluing the muzzle break

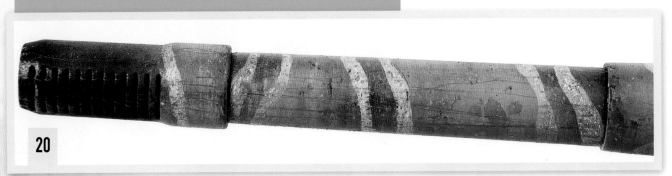

PHOTO 21 AND 22:
Super glue, accelerator and sheet plastic can also quickly fill unwanted holes, wide gaps and notches as in photos 21 and 22.

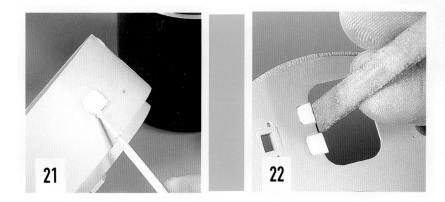

PHOTO 23 AND 24:
You can even fill holes using unwanted kit parts. In this case I simply glued the external fuel tank mount in place to fill the hole over a damaged area then cut it away. Weld detail was added representing where the part was once located.

These are the primary methods that I use for filling pin marks and unwanted gaps. Let's continue with the construction of this JSU-152 discussing more techniques for gluing parts.

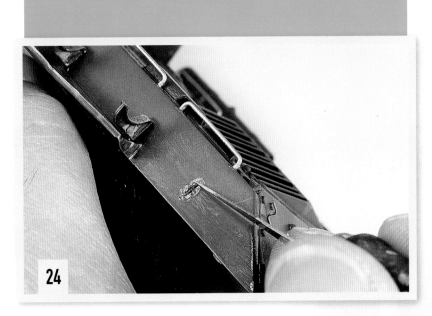

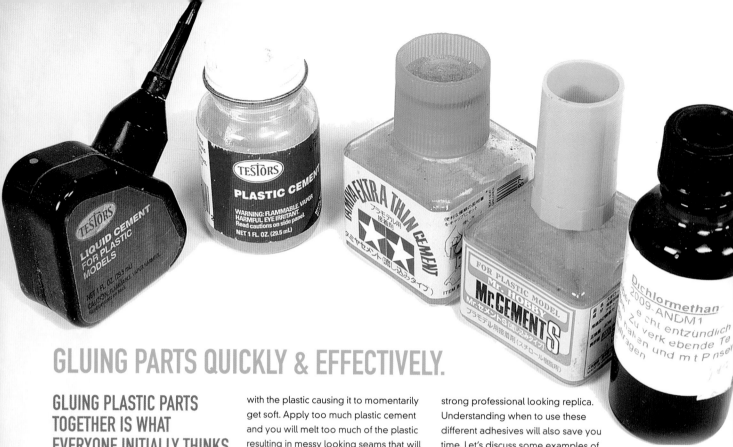

GLUING PARTS QUICKLY & EFFECTIVELY.

GLUING PLASTIC PARTS TOGETHER IS WHAT EVERYONE INITIALLY THINKS OF WHEN BUILDING MODELS.

It sounds easy but there are some things that you should know and keep in mind. Plastic cement is the tried and true glue used for assembling plastic models. This adhesive chemically reacts

with the plastic causing it to momentarily get soft. Apply too much plastic cement and you will melt too much of the plastic resulting in messy looking seams that will be evident through the paint on your finished replica.

There are many different types of plastic cements on the market containing different properties. Having some knowledge of these glues will help to ensure you a clean

strong professional looking replica. Understanding when to use these different adhesives will also save you time. Let's discuss some examples of these adhesives as we continue the assembly of the JSU-152.

PHOTO 3 THROUGH 4:
Thinner glues dry quicker giving you les time to reposition parts. They can give you a good bond quicker than thicker glues. Thinner glues also react less with the plastic reducing loss of fine detail on smaller fragile parts.

PHOTO 1 AND 2:
Let's start with viscous glues. Thick plastic adhesives dry slowly. This characteristic can be an advantage giving you ample time to reposition and align parts when needed such as these torsion bars. But again, these types of glue dry slowly. After using a straight edge to help align the torsion bars I needed to put the chasses down for about 24 hours to dry. Once dry I had a good strong bond.

PHOTO 5 AND 6:

Superglue is another important adhesive. Like plastic cement it comes in a variety of brands with slightly different properties. Modellers use super glue to attach metal photo etched parts and resin details. Most super glues dry rather quickly but can also be a bit messy and therefore noticeable through the paint if not carefully applied. Always have a good number of toothpicks handy for this task. The drying time for supper glue can be speeded up using accelerators. In fact, I use superglue and accelerators together for a number of tasks which I will explain more about later. I typically use both plastic cement and super glues together when assembling plastic models.

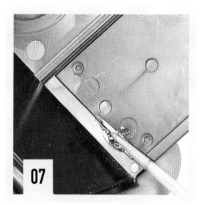

PHOTO 7:

I usually use superglue to quickly attach larger parts. Once everything is assembled and properly aligned I will then add liquid plastic cement in order to obtain stronger bonds between those parts.

PHOTO 8 THROUGH 10:

Some of the larger parts of a model such as the lower and upper hull for example, often need to have pressure applied in certain areas in order to line them up properly. This can be a result of poor kit design or distortion in the larger plastic pieces. As I mentioned, plastic cement obtains its bond by melting the plastic between the two details resulting in a slow drying time. If the parts do not fit properly you might need to hold them together for a long period of time with clamps while the plastic cement sets.

Small amounts of super glue, when carefully located, can hold larger parts together within minutes. When assembling the JSU-152 I put together most of the larger parts of the hull and superstructure using fine amounts of super glue. In photo ten I applied the super glue into this difficult to reach corner using a hobby knife. Once the major parts were properly assembled I brushed liquid plastic cement into all of the grooves. The capillary action of the seams will absorb the liquid cement giving you a stronger cleaner bond once it's had ample time to dry.

Although great for gluing model parts I use plastic cement to also obtain various effects. Some of these examples are replicating flame-cut edges and texturing. Let's continue with flame-cut edges.

FLAME CUT EDGES

I NORMALLY ASSEMBLE ARMOUR MODELS.

The actual vehicles they represent are comprised from heavy plates of steel and therefore flame-cut edges are always present. Flame cut edges are not always detailed authentically or even at all on plastic model kits. Let's take a look at some examples I have photographed while visiting different museums.

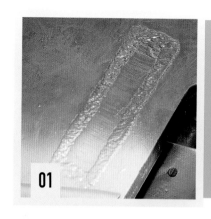

01

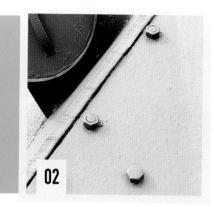

02

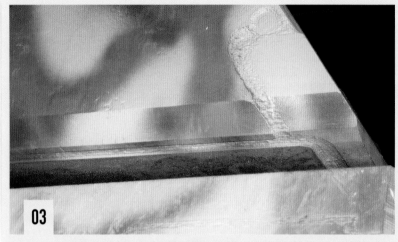

03

PHOTO 1 AND 2:
The texture of flame cut edges can vary rather drastically. On this Tiger II we can see the end of the rear plate protruding through the side plate. It has a rather smooth flame cut edge despite its thickness. Photo two is another example of a relatively smooth flame cut edge on the edge of this T-34 hull plate.

PHOTO 3
See how the ends of these enormous plates appear to have been machined on this German Maus Super Heavy Tank displayed in the Kabinka tank museum outside of Moscow. Please note that I have seen what certainly appear to be flame cut edges in photos of unassembled Maus turrets taken after the war.

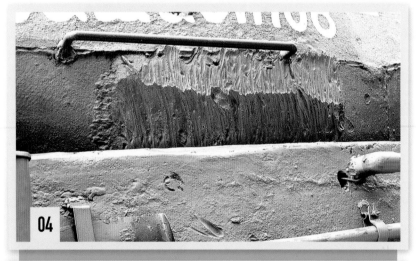

04

PHOTO 4 THROUGH 6:
Flame cut edges can very more drastically. "Ridiculous" is a word that came to my mind when viewing the flame cut edges of this Soviet JS-2. Even a reputable plastic model company like Tamiya rarely captures the essence of this rough texture.

05

06

PHOTO 7 AND 8:

The process I use to create these edges is rather simple. I simply run my hobby knife perpendicular across the edge making small slices as shown in photo number seven. After all you will need to do is simply apply liquid cement over the sliced edge. I have obtained average results using rotary tools but felt myself to have less control then when using a hobby knife and plastic cement.

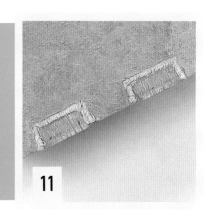

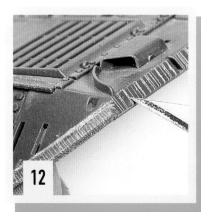

PHOTO 9 THROUGH 11:

 The edges of these rather thick dovetails on this E-75 are another example. The linier texture of flame-cut edges can be rather random. You will need to press harder and sometimes even turn your knife sideways to obtain these thicker grooves. You can even add more glue, let the piece sit for a bit, then make some more slices in the edge. Note the authenticity of the random assortment of lighter and heavy slices.

PHOTO 12 THROUGH 15:

The JS-3 seen throughout this book has a number of flame-cut edges. Some are much rougher than others. The edges of the lower front hull plate are rather smooth while the ends of the upper plates are much more dramatic.

One cannot deny that the rough look of the flame cut edges on this JS-3 greatly add to its menacing appearance. As with most art forms sometimes it's the little things that can really contribute to the final overall appearance of a project. The same can be said for the next topic that we will discuss. Let's move onto texturing cast surfaces.

BASIC TEXTURING

TEXTURING IS RATHER EASY.

It is a great way of adding life to a scale model. Well applied textures can give an impression of weight while adding contrast between different parts and details. In this segment we will go through a few examples for applying different types of texture onto plastic surfaces. In our first example we will look at a rather easy case using steps that I employ onto almost every model I construct. The second example is a bit more involved requiring some preparation. Let's begin by looking at a few examples of different textures.

PHOTO 1 AND 2:
As with most other processes that go into both the model assembly and finishing steps I usually begin by first referencing a number of different photos. Pictures one through five were taken in a few of the museums I have visited in and around Moscow. Textures will obviously vary on different components of various vehicles. Textures will also differ between the same components such as turret castings for example. The first turret of these two T-34/85 tanks was photographed in Kubinka. Note its rather milder cast texture when compared to the second example photographed in the outskirts of Moscow. Differences in textures as seen on these two examples allow modellers options in the type of surface that we would like to have on our finished model. Personally I prefer rougher textures because they look more menacing while contrasting with the smoother rolled steel plates on the vehicle. Of course other modellers may prefer smoother castings.

PHOTO 3 AND 4:
Textures can differ on rolled steel plates as well. Note that the front plates of this Ferdinand in photo 3 are rather smooth. These thick plates on the sides of this Maus prototype are more pitted with laminations. It is good to note that the plates located on the side of the Maus are considerably thicker than those of the Ferdinand. Therefore, as with castings, some research should also be undertaken when constructing models with armoured plates.

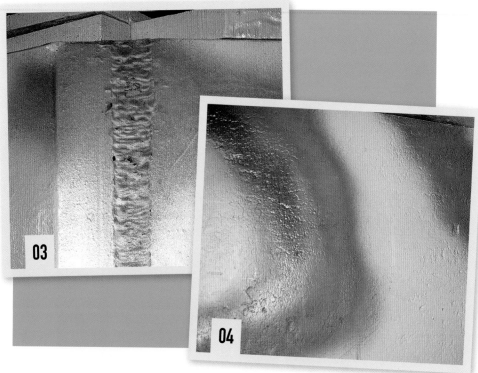

PHOTO 5:
This mantlet of an SU-100 is another good example of a typical cast surface. Note that it contains some small fragment impacts on the lower side as well as on the underside of the gun.

PHOTO 6 THROUGH 10:
Adding texture over a surface can be rather basic. My method is the same on most heavily armoured subjects. Tamiya putty thinned with a slow drying liquid cement is all that I usually use along with a couple of old brushes for application. After letting the putty dry for about a day or so I will then lightly smoothen the surface with sandpaper using a circular polishing motion. The E-75 and the JS-3 are two examples of simple texturing on heavily armoured plates.

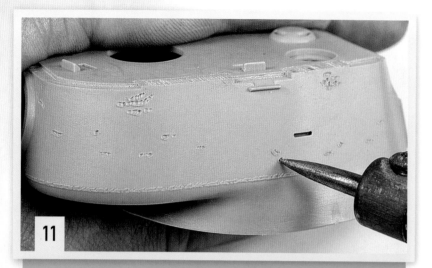

» PHOTO 11 AND 12:

In this next example we will texture a plastic Russian KV-1 turret. Texturing this turret was more involved but still rather straightforward as you will see. Often some preparation is needed before texturing. Prior to adding putty I had to apply a few laminations and pits into the turret to represent some typical flaws that I have observed on sand castings. A hot pointed soldering iron can quickly be used for this task.

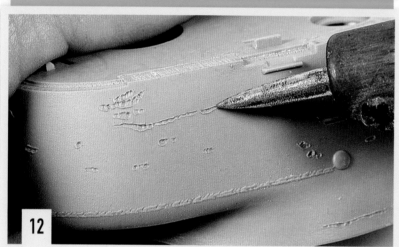

PHOTO 13:

I also decided to add other textures such as flame cut edges at this time. Adding weld detail will be discussed later.

PHOTO 14 THROUGH 16:

Similar work needed to be done to the mantlet. I have noticed that the mantlets of KV tanks contain a very rough cut on the right edge where the iron sprue was removed while the opposite edge is relatively smooth. A very random rough flame cut edge was added using slices with my hobby knife. I also added a few random small slices on the opposite side. Next I slightly reduced the texture by sanding each side down a little. More pits were added again using the soldering iron.

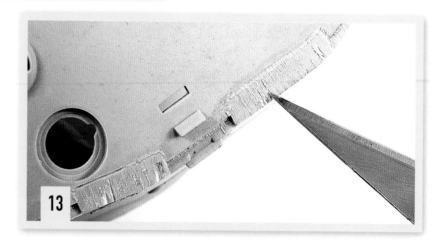

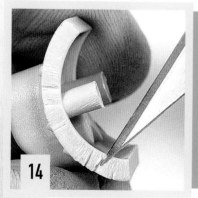

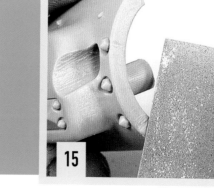

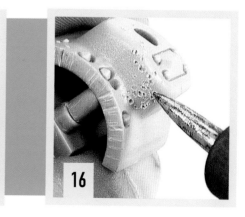

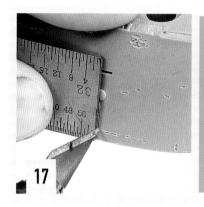
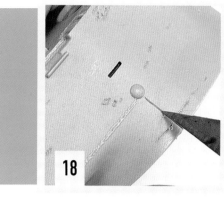
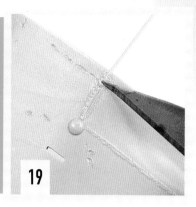

PHOTO 17 THROUGH 19:

 I feel that the seams on the Trumpeter turret are a bit too even and rather boring. You will also need to add another vertical seam on each side. These two seams were added by first slicing a groove in the turret with the aid of a straight edge. Stretched sprue was then applied, softened with liquid cement, then textured using a hobby knife.

PHOTO 20 AND 21:

 More details to represent what may have been flaws in the sand casting were added using small lengths of stretched sprue and liquid cement. I have also observed details such as these in photos.

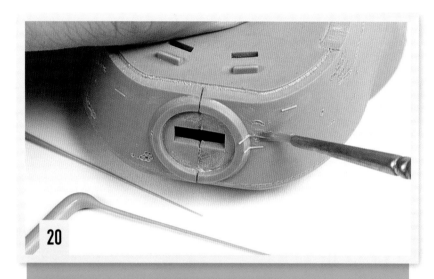

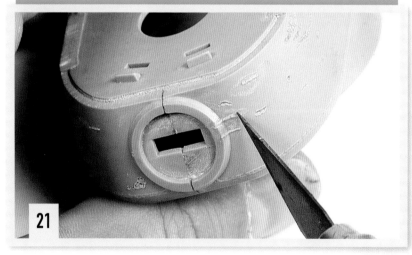

PHOTO 22 THROUGH 24:

There are two large flame cut edges where the sprues from the casting process were located on the lower rear of the cast KV turrets. These flame cut edges are not present on the Trumpeter models. First I needed to build up these areas. I made a few basic shapes from sheet plastic then glued them onto the proper locations.

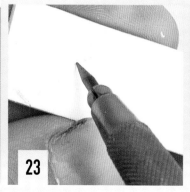
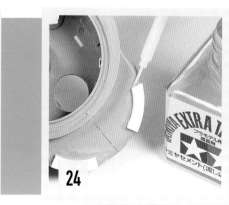

PHOTO 25 THROUGH 29:
There are a few different brands of two-part epoxy putties on the market preferred by modellers. Apoxie Sculpt has always been one of my favorites. I started using this brand frequently a number of years ago when constructing masters and still depend on it very much today for a variety of tasks. In these photos I used the Apoxie Sculpt to fill the gaps between the plastic and the lower fillets of the turret. Wet your finger with water to aid when spreading and smoothening the putty.

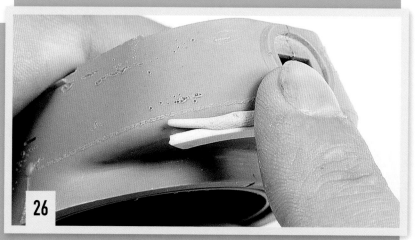

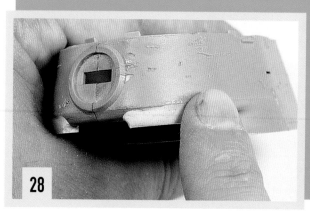

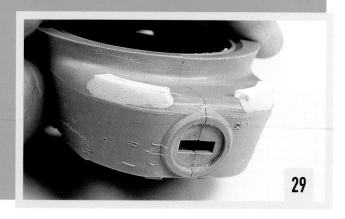

PHOTO 30 THROUGH 32:
Once the putty had some time to solidify I sized and beveled the extruded pieces of sheet plastic using a rigid flat sander. Again I used my hobby knife to add the flame cut edges.

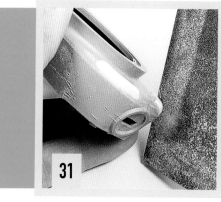

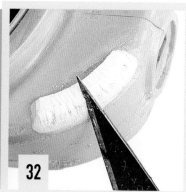

PHOTO 33 THROUGH 36:
It was now time to start adding the Tamiya putty. This time I added a coat of larger random clumps less saturated with glue. After letting the first thick random coat dry for about 10 to 15 minutes I applied more putty this time thinned further with liquid glue connecting all of the areas from the first coat.

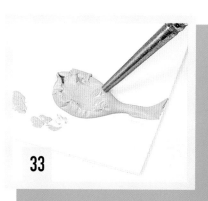

PHOTO 37 AND 38:
You might need to rapidly tap some areas with the brush in order to obtain the random texture that you are looking for. You will also find that some of the areas of thicker putty will dry to a convincing finish without the need of any added manipulation with the brush.

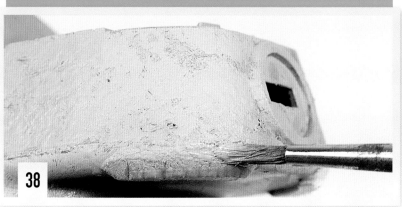

PHOTO 39 AND 40:

A finer brush was needed for texturing the mantlet to help insure that none of the putty was accidently brushed onto any of the details I wanted kept smooth, such as the bolts. I felt that the glue and putty had softened the flame cut edges too much on the turret top. I decided to retexture these areas agian using my hobby knife. You will often need to go back and forth between various techniques in order to get the final result that you are content with.

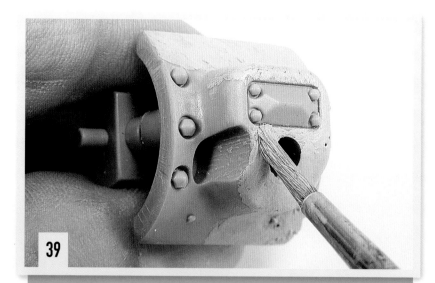

39

PHOTO 41 THROUGH 43:

When viewing the photos of the completed turret you can see that the casting seams, pits and other flaws that I added, although softer, are still visible though the layers of putty.

Note that the subtle random textured sides of the turret and mantlet have an interesting contrast with the top of the turret and gun adding more life to the piece.

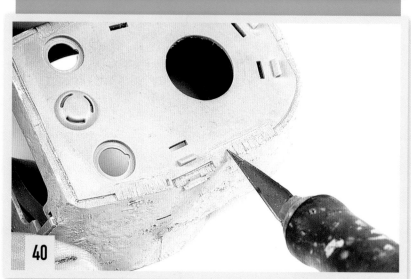

40

41

42

43

There are other materials, such as fine sand for example, that can aid you in obtaining fine textures. The materials used in this chapter are easy to find and the techniques demonstrated rather simple to apply.

Please note that rust can sometimes give an inaccurate textured appearance on old museum pieces that have been recently painted again for display. I have noticed this on vehicles on exhibition in Russia that have been pulled from swamps and rivers. Try to keep this in mind when studying photos for reference.

SIMPLE, EFFECTIVE BATTLE DAMAGE

WITH THE EXCEPTION TO A VERY GOOD FINISH, NOTHING ADDS MORE AUTHENTICITY TO A MODEL THEN WELL APPLIED BATTLE DAMAGE.

Battle damage does not need to be all that drastic and the methods used to create it can be rather simple. A heat source such as a cigarette lighter and small blunt object is all that would be needed to carefully add a similar dent into a plastic idler wheel as seen in this photograph to the right. This simple effect would add character to a model of a KV tank.

Remember that the model's finish needs to be considered during construction. Damaged parts can influence the weathering steps enhancing a finished model as I will show you momentarily. Thoughtfully applied battle damage can even sometimes allow you to completely change the appearance of your replica. The JS-3 seen throughout this book is a good example. Removing the sheet metal components exposing the inverted sloped armour on one side allowed me to present this popular subject rather differently. We will be discussing more about the methods used to construct the JS-3 in the upcoming sections.

Prior to simulating any type of damage on a model I would strongly recommend that you study photos of the actual vehicle first. Like with weathering effects, battle damage can also be easily overdone. Most of the time I will just apply a number of damaged effects that I observed on three to five different vehicles on to one model.

I am going to move on with the construction of this JSU-152 by discussing some rather simple methods used to damage plastic fenders. Although the fenders in the single photo that I found of this particular vehicle were all intact I felt that damaging these elements would make the model more exciting. I have always enjoyed areas of intense weathering on a model. I knew that removing some of the fenders, such as the two located at the back of this JS-3 would have resulted in more earth being tossed up onto the rear. The different textures of the earth tones contrast nicely with the rather smooth satin finish.

PHOTO 1 THROUGH 4:

The rear fender comes moulded onto the upper hull of the Tamiya JSU-152 kit. After viewing some reference photos I carefully cut the part from the hull. The area of the fender where it would mate onto the lower rear plate was cut from the part. Next I removed the remaining unwanted plastic by sanding and slicing it away.

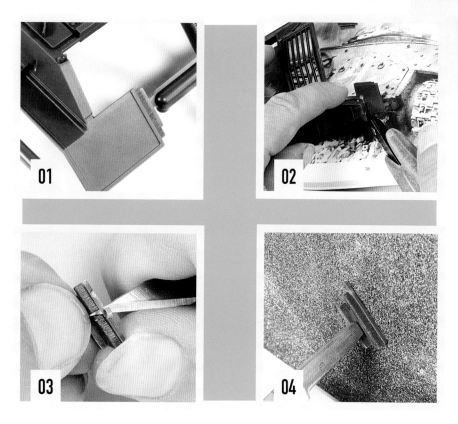

PHOTO 5 AND 6:

Flame-cut edges were re-scribed into the parts. The parts were then glued onto the proper locations on the lower rear plate.

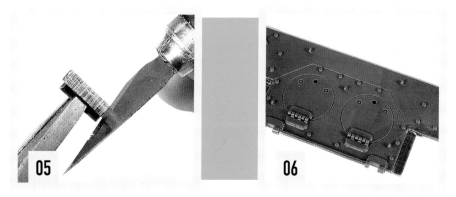

PHOTO 7 AND 8:

Other random sections of the fenders were also detached. First I carefully removed large sections using cutters

PHOTO 9 THROUGH 12:

Next a sharp knife was used to remove the left over unwanted sections of plastic. Various sanding tools were used to finish cleaning the sides of the hull and superstructure. Further crimps and bends can be carefully added into thin plastic parts using flat pliers.

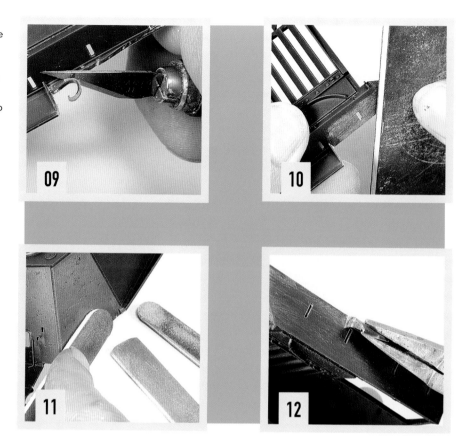

PHOTO 13 AND 14:

Like with the rear fenders, I needed to also cut and clean a section of the front one then glue it onto its proper location. As I mentioned, studying photos is important.

These fenders were separate assemblies and some components of these parts might still remain on the vehicle after they are broken away. Sometimes small parts need to be cut, cleaned, then glued back onto the model

PHOTO 15 THROUGH 17:

Try to keep battle damage random. The larger sections of fenders were only removed from one side of the vehicle and small dents placed onto the ones on the other side. The completed model in photo 17 shows the added mud effects that could be present as a result of the missing fenders.

As I have shown the methods for creating battle damage on models built from the box can be rather simple. Battle damage also affects the weathering process proving that the type of finish does start with assembly therefore careful planning is necessary. Let's now continue with this JSU-152 with discussing a bit about grab handles.

15

16

17

SIMPLE GRAB HANDLES

GRAB HANDLES IN THE NEWER KITS ON THE MARKET ARE FAIRLY ACCURATE IN DIAMETER.

In the older, low-end kits they can have large seams making them oblong once the part has been cleaned. Details like grab handles are fragile parts and can easily be broken while handling during the painting of the model. Most modellers today opt to use stronger, cleaner formed wire replacements.

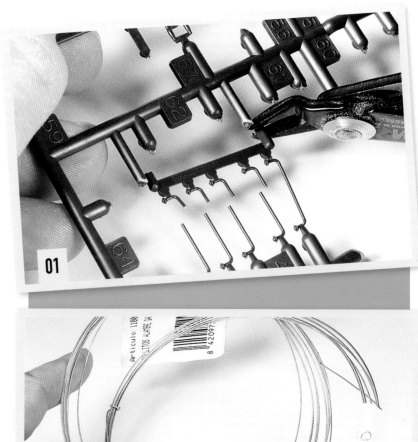

PHOTO 1 AND 2:

A few of the grab-handles in my JSU kit were broken. This might have been due to all of the stuff on my unorganized work bench. I broke the remaining ones while trying to remove them from the sprue. It will be handy for you to have a box of various diameter wires at your disposal for different types of detailing.

PHOTO 3 AND 4:

Pin vises and drill bits are also important. You will need them for a number of tasks ranging from wiring lights to detailing parts and adding grab-handles. The bronze coloured pin vise is great for firmly holding fine bits. The silver type that can be purchased in most hobby stores tend to wear out over time losing their ability to grip the finer diameter bits. After you choose some wire that is to the correct diameter find a bit with the same width and drill holes through the plastic in all of the locations that the grab handles are to be located on the kit.

PHOTO 5 AND 6:

There are tools available to help quickly form grab handles. The one in the photo works pretty well. A strong flat object such as this straight edge will help in insure tight 90 degree bends. You can also use a set of pliers but the width of your grab handles will vary.

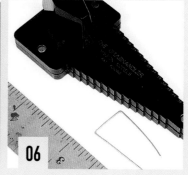

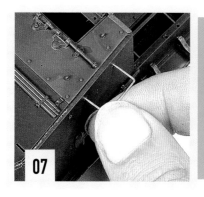 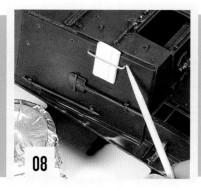 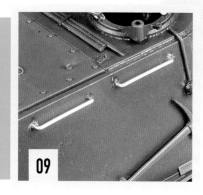

PHOTO 7 THROUGH 9:
Slide the formed handles into the holes you drilled earlier and use a spacer such as a piece of plastic to help you locate them while the glue is applied.

PHOTO 10 AND 11:
I also rebuilt the mounts for securing the tow cables onto the rear of the JSU using wire. I added an extra bend to be inserted and glued into a hole for added strength.

PHOTO 12:
Creating your own grab handles from wire is relatively basic but effective. They are plenty strong and will not break while you are handling the model during the rest of the assembly and painting processes. You can even add some damage to them as shown in photo 12.

Very similar methods can also be used for applying wiring detail to headlights horns and other components as I will show you next.

WIRING LIGHTS AND OTHER DETAILS

SOME MODELLERS DON'T BOTHER WITH WIRING HEADLIGHTS.

They are very small fixtures that one might not feel to be worth the extra time practically on a model such as this. Sometimes I tend to agree if I have a tight deadline to complete an article for example. If you do have the time I would recommend you taking a few moments to add them. Fine details like this do add a bit more realism to the finished model. In fact judges will demerit a model which does not have the components such as the headlights and horn wired. This is something to note if you are interested in entering your work in competitions at shows.

Wires are very fine details. You need to glue them onto the components firmly but also cleanly in order not to cover any of the detail. During this segment I will show you a few tricks

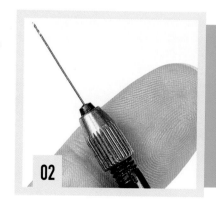

PHOTO 1:
As I have already stated, it will be in your best interest to have a selection of various diameter wire at your disposal for tasks like this. Soldering wire is also a great medium for making wire details. It is best to drill fine holes to insert the wire into. I recommend finding a pin vice that will hold the finest bits. You'll want to have a number of these fine drills on hand. Although fairly inexpensive, they can break rather easily.

PHOTO 2 AND 3:
How you place the bit into the pin vise is important. Fine bits will quickly break when left sticking far out of the vice like seen in photo 2.

Placing the bit as far as you can into pin vise as shown in photo 3 will drastically reduce the possibility of snapping it.

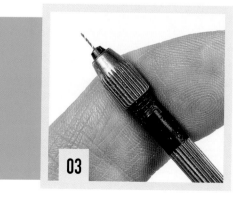

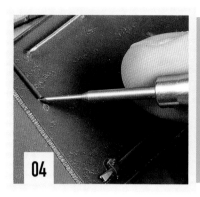

04

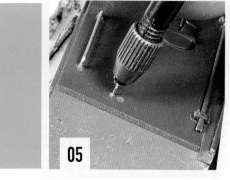

05

PHOTO 6:

I super glued lengths of wire into the holes that I drilled into the lights. Some of the parts are still connected to the sprue for better ease of handling while drilling the holes. Once the wire was firmly glued I removed the rest of the sprues and finished cleaning the parts.

PHOTO 4 AND 5:

Make a small puncture in the plastic using a pointed object such as this panel scriber. This will work as a small pilot hole for you to start drilling through the plastic.

PHOTO 7 THROUGH 9:

After the superglue had some time to dry I inserted the wires through the holes that I drilled into the superstructure and pulled the wire tight from the inside. Next I glued the lights into place then super glued the wires on the inside.

06

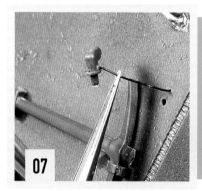

07

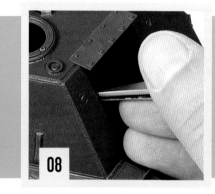

08

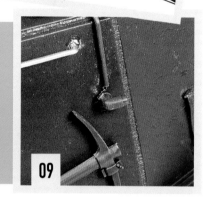

09

PHOTO 10 THROUGH 13:

I decided to wire the front light and horn a bit differently. There was a small electrical junction for wiring these components at the front of the JSU-152. I made this part using a length of plastic rod with a piece of wire through one end. I drilled a hole through the superstructure, inserted the rod, and glued it from the inside. The light and horn were also glued at this time. Once the glue had time to dry I cut the wire to a correct size and inserted it into the small holes I drilled earlier.

Wiring the headlights were the final details needed to finish assembling the hull and superstructure of the JSU-152. Now I needed to assemble and fit the plastic tracks included with the kit. Let's now look at some techniques that can be used to assemble tracks.

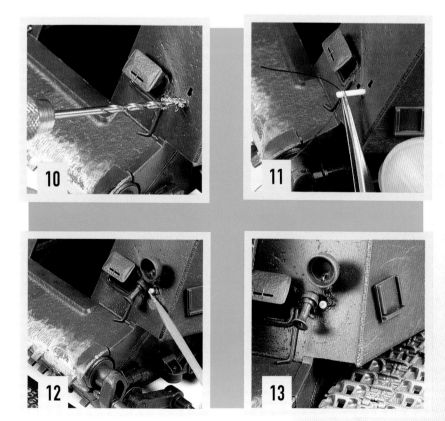

10

11

12

13

ASSEMBLING TRACK

TRACKS ARE ONE OF THE KEY DETAILS WHICH MAKE ARMOUR MODELS SO ENJOYABLE AND APPEALING FOR AFV ENTHUSIASTS.

The tracks and running gear can sometimes cover an area that takes up to around one third or more of the model's surface. Therefore it is imperative that the tracks be treated with much care during assembly in order to make them look natural. Tracks that are inadequately put together can really reduce the appearance of a completed replica. Actually, it is the tracks that I often look at first in order to quickly start forming an understanding of the overall level of skill that was put into a completed model that I am observing when judging.

Most armour model kits now come with the plastic link-by-link tracks that are rather good.

In the past decades modellers had to work with the older "rubber-band" style flexible plastic tracks which have now become rather less common. Some of this is due to their often limited detail and lack of natural sags over the return rollers although there are some methods to obtain this. Rubber band tracks are of course the easiest types to assemble as it only takes gluing each of the ends end together and placing them onto the running gear. The AFV Club T-49 tracks used on this Sherman were ideal for this project. The lack of sags over the return rollers are hidden by the side plates. They took me only five minutes to assemble.

We will be assembling three different runs of tracks. We will start with the plastic individual linked tracks found in most injection moulded kits today. Next we will assemble some Workable Modelkasten tracks. In the third segment we will discuss and assemble some Friulmodel workable metal tracks. There are many types of tracks available from a number of different companies. The ones covered here are the types most commonly used and which I also have the most hours of experience with.

ASSEMBLING PLASTIC TRACK

PLASTIC TRACK LINKS PROVIDED IN TODAY'S MODEL KITS LOOK PRETTY CONVINCING.

Assembling these injection moulded links isn't really too difficult depending upon both the model and size of the links. You also cannot beat the price considering that you can usually pay around half the cost of the kit or more for a decent set of after-market replacements. The main problems encountered with kit provided links is that they usually contain pin marks that should be filled. As you will see it is not too difficult. Let's continue with preparing and assembling the plastic track links included with the JSU-152.

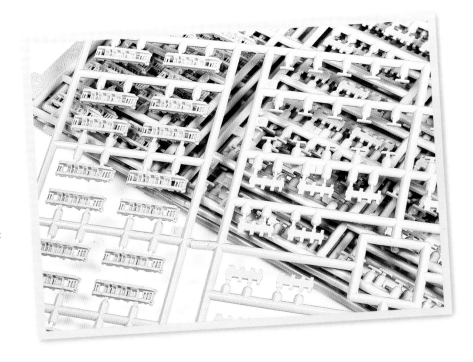

 PHOTO 1 AND 2:
The track links included inside of the Tamiya JSU-152 kit are rather large making them easy to both handle and clean. A jig is also included to help you assemble the sagged runs that go across the tops of the return-rollers. After cutting the link from the sprues I used a flat sander to quickly remove the seams on each end of the links.

 PHOTO 3 AND 4:
The problem with plastic tracks included with model kits is that there are often pin marks in each link usually on the inner sides. Super glue and accelerator are the fastest means that I know of for fixing this problem.

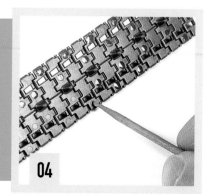

 PHOTO 5 AND 6:
After filling the holes the super glue was sanded smooth. Make sure you finish cleaning by polishing the tracks using fine sand paper. I saved a bit of time by only filling the pin marks on the lower visible parts of the treads.

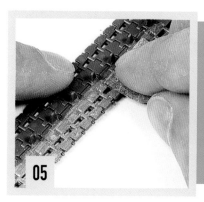

07

08

09

PHOTO 7 THROUGH 9:
The jig included for the top runs of track really helped to save time insuring proper sags between the return rollers. The little spacers on the jig were in the way of the teeth on the links and needed to be cut away.

Unequally deposited amounts of glue will cause distortion in the lengths of track. Reduce this problem by applying the liquid glue onto the center of the links. Once the glue had about 15 minutes to dry I slid them into place over the return rollers.

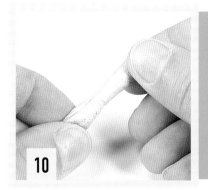

10

11

12

PHOTO 10 THROUGH1 12:
Takk was used to temporarily hold the bottom runs in place. I used paper shims to keep the upper tracks

pressed against the return rollers while the glue had time to completely dry overnight.

PHOTO 13 THROUGH1 15:
I kept the upper and lower runs of track secured so I could start assembling the four ends that would curl around the idler wheels and drive sprockets. Glue the tracks with a viscous slow drying cement that will give you time to properly form the runs around the sprocket and idler wheels.

Do not be shy with the Takk. Use it when ever and where ever possible in order to firmly hold

the runs of track in place while the glue holding the links together dries. The runs were not glued to each other at this time. Let the plastic cement dry for about a day then remove the track. You will need to make a note of which is the right and left hand sections of track. Due to the positioning of the torsion bars the locations of the road wheels were different on each side of the JS tanks. After painting if you mix up the lengths of track when gluing them the sags will not be on-center between the return rollers. This will severely subtract from the final

appearance of the model. Techniques for painting these tracks will be discussed in book 2. Finishing the construction of this JSU-152 will conclude the fundamental assembly methods in this first book. Again, if you can master all of these methods you are well on your way.

13

14

15

ASSEMBLING WORKABLE MODELKASTEN TRACKS

THERE ARE A FEW COMPANIES THAT SPECIALIZE IN AFTER-MARKET INJECTION MOULDED TRACK LINKS.

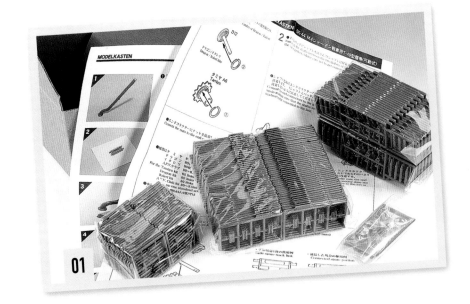

Modelkasten from Japan is one of the more popular ones. Their kits contain many sprues and assembling one run can take some time. Most of the Modelkasten injection moulded sets are designed to be workable so much care should be taken when placing the glue during assembly. Runs of tracks such as these are also very fragile. Despite these concerns many modellers prefer Modelkasten track sets over others because of their good reputation for quality and accuracy.

PHOTO 1 THROUGH 3:
These M4 T-49 tracks are an example of how complex and detailed Modelkasten sets can be. Each separate link, once assembled, will contain eight to ten parts. The Tiger I track links that we will be putting together in this example are more of a standard type Modelkasten set that you will encounter. For this example let's assemble a small run of 15 links.

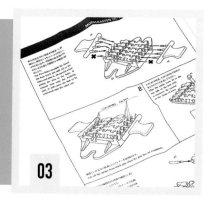

PHOTO 4 AND 5:
The first thing that you will want to do is cut all of the links form the sprues and clean them. The "fingers" that join the tracks are cleverly attached to these little handles allowing you to insert them into the ends of the links connecting five of them at a time. Add just a bit of glue to the ends of each finger being careful not to stick the links together. Use viscose glue for this task. If your liquid glue is too thin it might get pulled between the pieces by capillary action gluing the links rendering them unmovable.

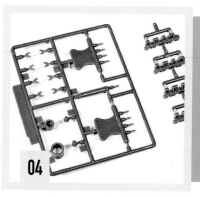

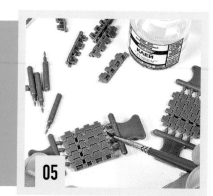

PHOTO 6 AND 7:
After letting the glue set for a few hours I cut the fingers from the handles and cleaned the ends.

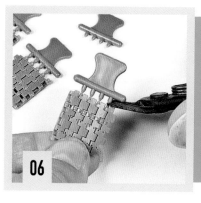

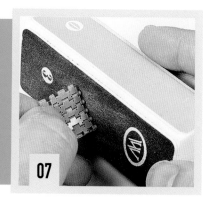

PHOTO 8 THROUGH 11:

I cut the horns from the sprues as shown. Leaving a bit of the sprue gave me a nice handle to help place these small parts. After cutting the remainder of the sprues away it was also easier to clean the ends of all the horns while they were firmly attached to the runs.

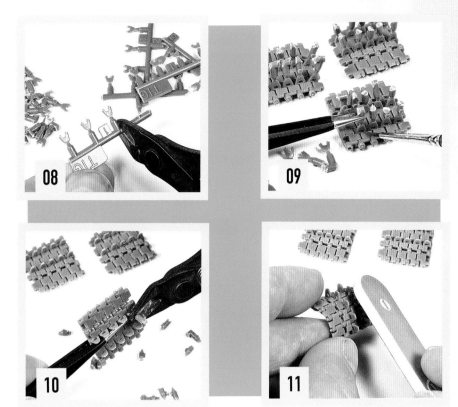

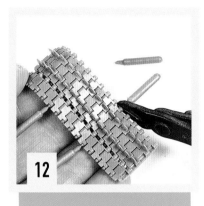

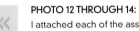

PHOTO 12 THROUGH 14:

I attached each of the assembled runs together using the single fingers also included on the sprues. I let the glue dry then cut the handles away. The Modelkasten set used on this VK45.02 was even simpler because the horns were moulded into each link. Only the fingers needed to be assembled connecting the links.

ASSEMBLING METAL TRACKS

FRIULMODEL, MANUFACTURED IN HUNGARY, ARE TODAY SOME OF THE MOST COMMONLY USED AFTER-MARKET TRACKS

They are made out of metal and assembled with wire. Friulmodel tracks are workable and fairly easy to both put together and wrap around the running gear of an AFV model. Assembled runs of Friulmodel tracks are both heavy and strong. This weight results in nice natural looking sags between the return rollers for example as seen on this KV-1.

Their strength also allows for heavy weathering that will not cause the links to fall apart when wrapping them around the running gear. Friulmodel tracks are a bit expensive. As I said they are also heavy. In fact they could literally double the weight of your model but this could also be an advantage. As the old saying goes, "It's got weight".

PHOTO 1 THROUGH 3:
Most of the Friulmodel sets are relativity straight forward as in the case of these Tiger II tracks. These links and horns are cast as one part and only need to be assembled with the included wire. No superglue is necessary on these simpler sets.

A few Friulmodel sets are more complicated and patience is needed when assembling them. This set for the Tiger II/Hunting Tiger is one of those examples. There are three different bags enclosed containing different links and connectors along with lengths of brass wire. Also included is a jig to aid with assembly. Some Friulmodel sets also include metal drive sprockets to replace the less accurate ones found in older kits.

PHOTO 4 THROUGH 6:
Some tools will also be needed for assembly. First you should inspect each link removing any flash. This is important because not doing so could affect the assembly. You might see as you start inserting the wire that some of the holes, as a result of poor casting, may need to be bored out using a fine drill roughly the diameter of the wire.

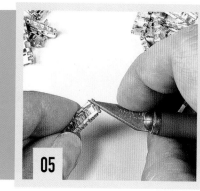

PHOTO 7 AND 8:
I used the jig to aid with the location of the parts

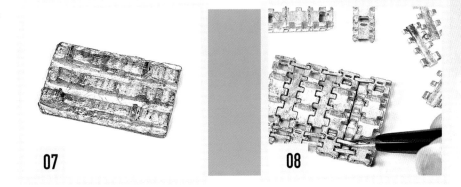

07

08

PHOTO 9 AND 10:
Friulmodel links are designed to have a friction fit. With the parts in place insert the wire as far as you can. Next use a set of side cutters to carefully grip the wire at about 2 millimeters from the track and finish pushing it through in small intervals at a time. It might be easier to hold the jig and parts together with your fingers to finish inserting the wire

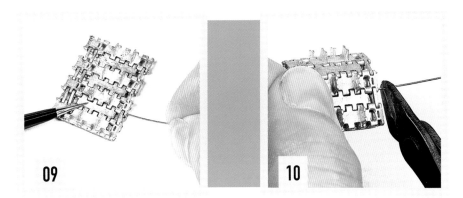

09

10

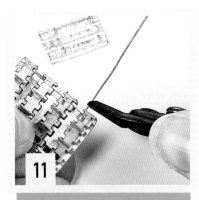

11

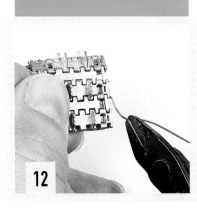

12

PHOTO 11 AND 12:
It's important that you do not push in the wire at a distance of more than 2 millimeters from the track. This will only cause the wire to buckle

PHOTO 13 THROUGH 15:
When assembling this set I occasionally ran into problems with getting the wire through the last small link. Tweezers were used to aid in positioning this part in order to properly slide the wire through.

With a bit of practice Friulmodel track sets are rather easy to assemble not requiring too much time. Sometimes you will run into problems with inserting the wire. This can quickly be fixed by running a small drill bit through the holes in the links. Methods for painting metal tracks will be covered in book 2.

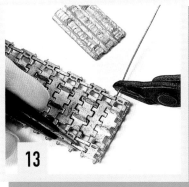

13

14

15

04 WORKING WITH RESIN PARTS

I HAVE PERSONALLY FOUND RESIN KITS AND ACCESSORIES TO BE A BIT OF A DOUBLE EDGED SWORD FOR ALL TYPES OF MODELLERS.

Most of us know the old saying, "you can smell the resin." Wasn't that phrase the truth during the 90s and through the beginning of the last decade when the next big show was fast approaching. Most people including myself have at one time enjoyed spending lots of money on resin after-market kits and accessories. Depending on what you choose to purchase you could be getting something rather nice or completely wasting your money on nothing more than junk.

Synthetic resin is a type of plastic that is poured into a silicone mold while in a liquid state (at room temperature) than solidifies permanently. Once solid the part can be removed and the silicone mold used again producing a finite amount of copies. Resin casting is used in numerous industries for limited production. Smaller after-market companies prefer casting parts in resin because the process is relatively inexpensive.

The resin kits and accessories on the market benefit scale modellers for a number of reasons. Resin accessories allow us to purchase accurate replacement parts allowing us to quickly improve details or correct mistakes found on injection-moulded kits. These accessories include an array of items such wheels, turrets, and other small accessories such as exhaust pipes.

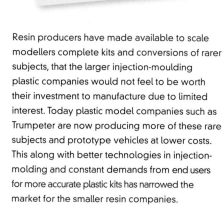

Resin producers have made available to scale modellers complete kits and conversions of rarer subjects, that the larger injection-moulding plastic companies would not feel to be worth their investment to manufacture due to limited interest. Today plastic model companies such as Trumpeter are now producing more of these rare subjects and prototype vehicles at lower costs. This along with better technologies in injection-molding and constant demands from end users for more accurate plastic kits has narrowed the market for the smaller resin companies.

You need to be selective when purchasing resin kits and accessories. The majority of these resin kit manufactures are very professional, but there can be exceptions. The hand made nature of these products means that there can sometimes be flaws due to damaged rubber moulds or missing parts so it is worth researching sometimes before making a purchase.

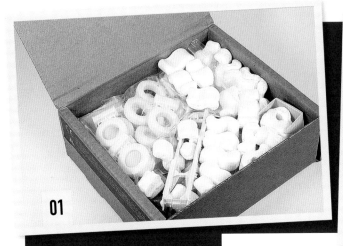

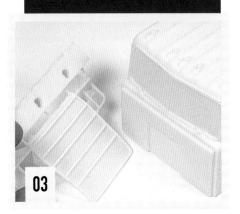

PHOTO 1 THROUGH 3

Before we discuss the techniques needed for working with cast resin parts lets quickly view one of the complete kits currently available. This U.S. Army M916 Tractor from Minimanfactory is a decent example of a good complete multimedia resin kit. The set I have was well packaged with all parts present. All of the thin delicate parts were also well cast with limited air bubbles, distortion and shrinkage often encountered in complex kits such as this.

Clear instructions and a photo etch fret are also included. Note the flash in photo three indicating where the mold needed to be cut in order to remove the parts. Unwanted parts from the casting proses such as the casting blocks and flash should be fairly easy to remove and clean if the kit has been designed well. Resin kits such as this are what all devoted hobbyists enjoy spending large amounts of their disposable income on. This is a good example of a hi-quality multimedia kit of a subject currently unavailable in plastic.

PHOTO 4

This Krupp Steyr Waffentrger is another example of a full resin kit that included workable metal tracks and a turned aluminum gun barrel. My kit went together rather well and contained a few flaws. Other modellers have since informed me that their examples of this same kit had numerous problems with poor casting and distortion in the larger components. I was probably lucky enough to get a kit produced from new molds. Quality of kits from the same reference produced by a company can also differ dramatically. Again, I would advise doing research about the company prior to spending large amounts of money. This kit is also now available in plastic by a much larger firm at less than half the price. A sign of the changing market for resin companies.

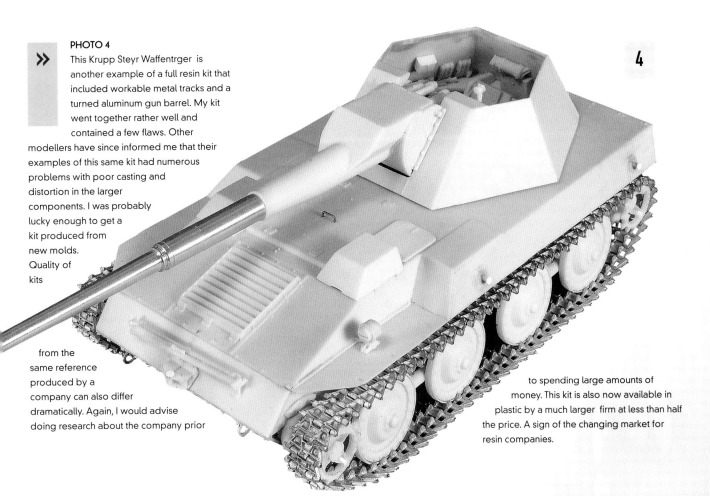

PHOTO 5 AND 6:

To discuss the methods used for cleaning resin parts. We will prepare this BT-7a turret from Complect ZIP. Complect ZIP is a small garage company from Russia.

PHOTO 7 THROUGH 10:

I started cleaning the turret by removing the flash on the bottom first with my knife and then wet sandpaper. Wet sandpaper will trap any dust caused while sanding resin parts. The dust created when working with resin should be controlled and disposed of safely. Avoid inhaling it and wash your hands after working with resin parts. The flash from all of the open areas was also removed.

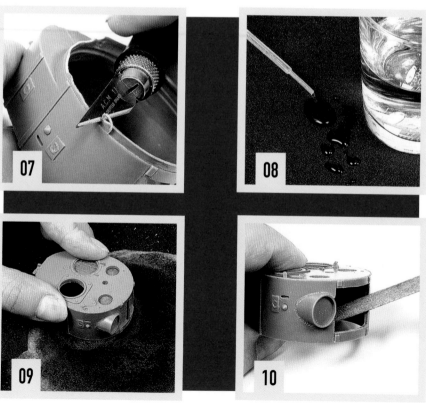

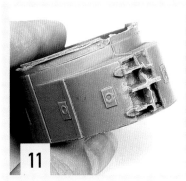

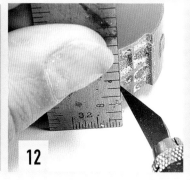

PHOTO 11 THROUGH 13:
The only major drawback with this conversion was the remnants of an ugly casting block located on the rear of the turret that needed to be removed. I started cleaning this area using a file. I needed to scribe two lines on each side of the opening to ensure clean flat edges for the door to mate up against. When I had scribed the lines to about the same depth as the rest of the opening I continued cleaning.

PHOTO 14 THROUGH 17:
Once content with the opening I had to rebuild the upper back part of the turret using sheet plastic. Superglue and accelerator were used to quickly fill any gaps. After cutting away the excess sheet plastic I sanded the remaining part flush with the rear of the turret. The superglue on the top was then sanded smooth.

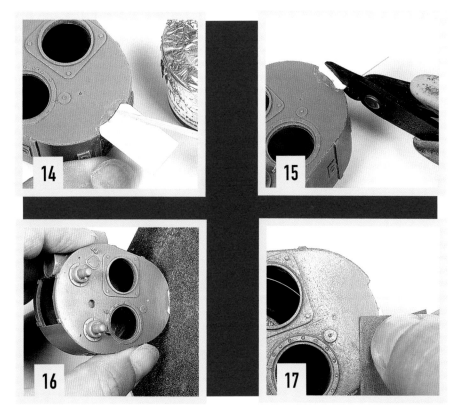

PHOTO 18 THROUGH 20:
The rear door was a bit short and needed to be built up using superglue and sheet plastic prior to being carefully glued into place.

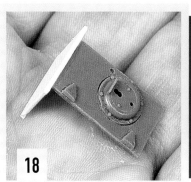

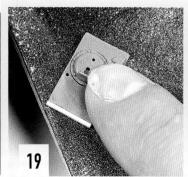

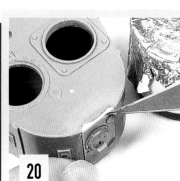

PHOTO 21 AND 22:

Gaps on each side of the door were filled using a two-part epoxy. I used my finger with water to smooth the putty before letting it dry and polishing it clean. The hinges attached to the turret needed to be rebuilt from plastic sheet

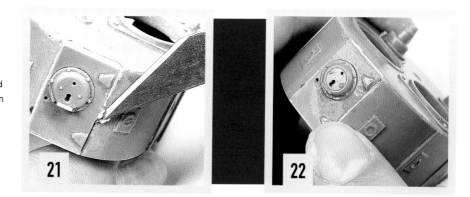

PHOTO 23 THROUGH 26:

Casting blocks can easily be removed using a razor saw. Once cut from the block you can simply eliminate the remaining injectors and flash using side cutters then finish cleaning it with sandpaper. Sharp hobby knifes are also good for removing casting blocks from fragile parts. Superglue has always been the best means for assembling resin parts. You should dry-fit all of the pieces first before using glue to ensure that everything fits properly.

Most of the tools and techniques discussed it this section should help you to clean and assemble most resin parts while correcting casting flaws often encountered in resin kits. Distortion of larger parts is also a common problem encountered in resin kits. I have solved this problem in the past by dipping the part in boiling water, reshaping it, then letting it cool for about ten minutes.

With the current availability of so many kits on the market the only resin parts that I now employ on my work are smaller detailed accessories to replace kit parts containing limited detail. What I do use a lot of these days are photo etch, sheet metal and other metallic parts which we'll come to soon.

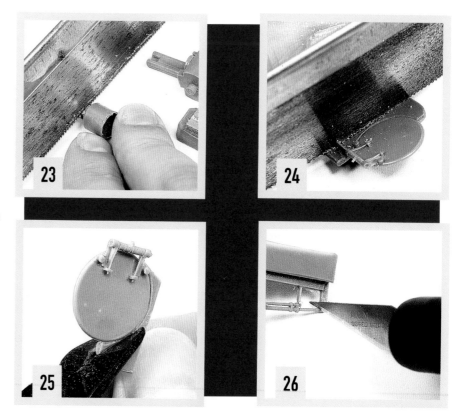

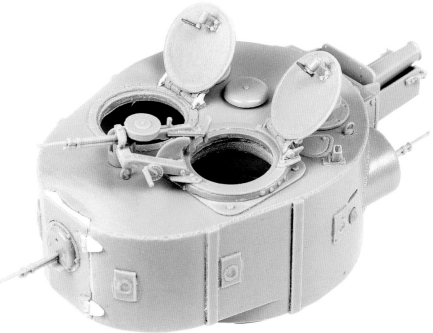

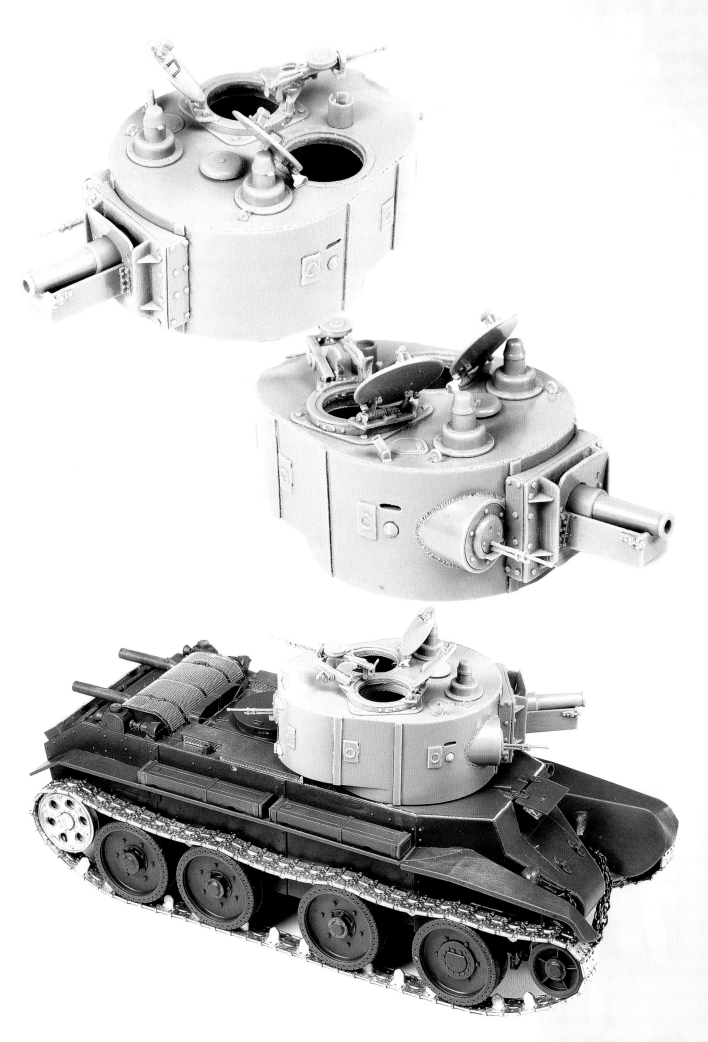

05 REMOVING SEGMENTS OF PLASTIC FROM KITS

01

AS YOU BECOME ACCUSTOMED TO THE FUNDAMENTAL SKILLS NEEDED FOR ASSEMBLING MORE COMPLEX MODELS IT WILL ONLY BE NORMAL THAT YOU FIND YOURSELF TAKING INTEREST IN AFTER-MARKET PARTS SUCH AS RESIN DETAILS, CONVERSIONS AND PHOTO-ETCH BRASS SETS.

Sometimes adding these parts can require the removal of large areas of the injection moulded kit.

Around 18 years ago when I first started modelling there were fewer kits available. To build any subject remotely obscure you would often need to purchase a conversion kit, often cast in resin, to mate with a plastic kit. Large areas of the injection moulded kit would often need to be removed in order to properly assemble it with the conversion. The first conversion that I attempted was a Jagd Panzer IV and I ruined two Academy kits before deciding that I had spent enough money. Today after years of practice I find removing large areas of plastic to be not only easy but even a bit therapeutic.

With awareness of proper tools, an understanding for the properties of the plastic and a bit of practice removing sections from injection moulded kits can be relatively easy. I will provide two examples in this section. The first example can be completed using a rotary tool followed by simple clean up using a flat file. The second example is more tedious requiring some skill and patience using different shaped files. Today there are a still a large number of conversions available along with endless PE (photo etch) kits that require the removal of sections from plastic kits. The examples in this segment will help you to develop both an awareness and understanding for the different tools and techniques available that will make cutting up your injection moulded kits less stressful and costly.

PHOTO 1 THROUGH 3:
In the first example we are going to remove the sides of a JS-3 in preparation for more authentic look copper sheet replacements. The primary apparatus needed for this fi task will be a rotary tool. Assorted different types of grinding bits and cut-off wheels are available for these devices. Althou a bit costly, one of these instruments along wit about a dozen different bits is very handy for multiple modelling tasks while lasting you a lifetime. Always use safety glasses when using these and similar electrical devices when modelling.

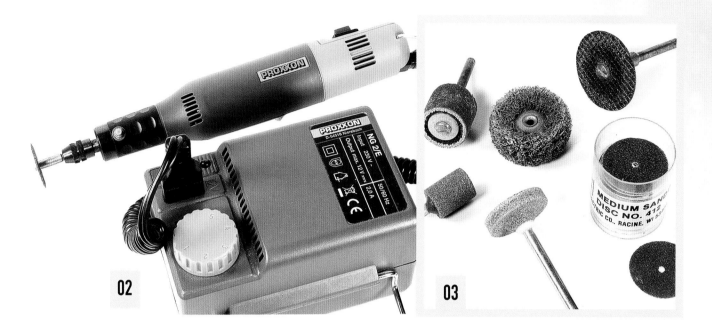

02

03

04

05

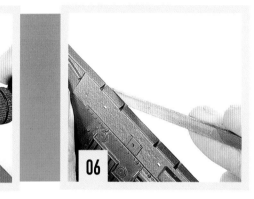

06

PHOTO 4 THROUGH 7:

The speed of most rotary tools can be adjusted. There are also adapters available to help you reduce the RPMs of these instruments. Friction from the bits and cut-off wheels will usually melt the plastic even at the lowest settings. Therefor it is important that you first make a "rough cut" leaving more or less 1/16th to 1/8th of an inch (1.5 to 3mm) as shown in photo three to avoid damaging the edges of the areas you will want present on the completed model. After completing a rough cut you can carefully remove any remaining unwanted bits of plastic using a flat a file.

07

PHOTO 8 AND 9:
Removing these E-75 grills required a little more patience and time. I started this chore by drilling a few holes and then widening and connecting them using a round file.

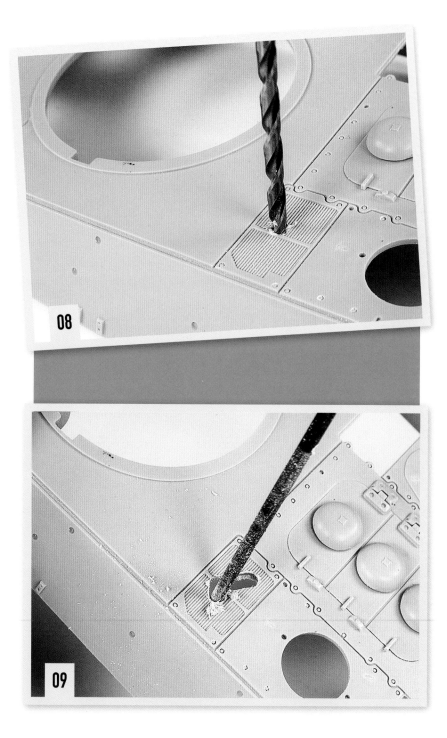

PHOTO 10 THROUGH 12:
Once there was enough room I switched over to a flat file and continued removing the plastic working out toward the sides of the moulded detail. Use the narrow sides of a flat file to grind away around details that you will want present once the part is removed.

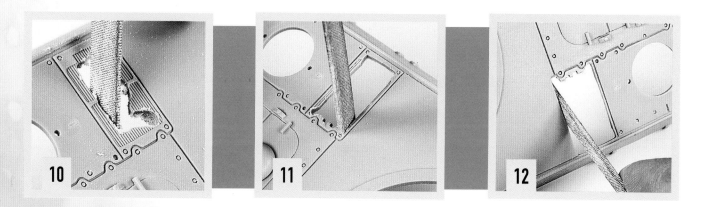

PHOTO 13 THROUGH 16:
To finish this example I used various shaped files to eliminate the unwanted areas around these rounded details. Once most of the unwanted plastic was removed I switched back to the flat file to carefully finish cleaning around the details.

The different examples for removing plastic details that could be displayed in this section are limitless. These two examples demonstrate that having an arsenal of various shaped files will really aid you with tasks such as these. Possessing a rotary tool will also help. To the contrary, sometimes you will find that large areas of plastic will need to be added to your replica. Let us again move onward to cladding large open areas.

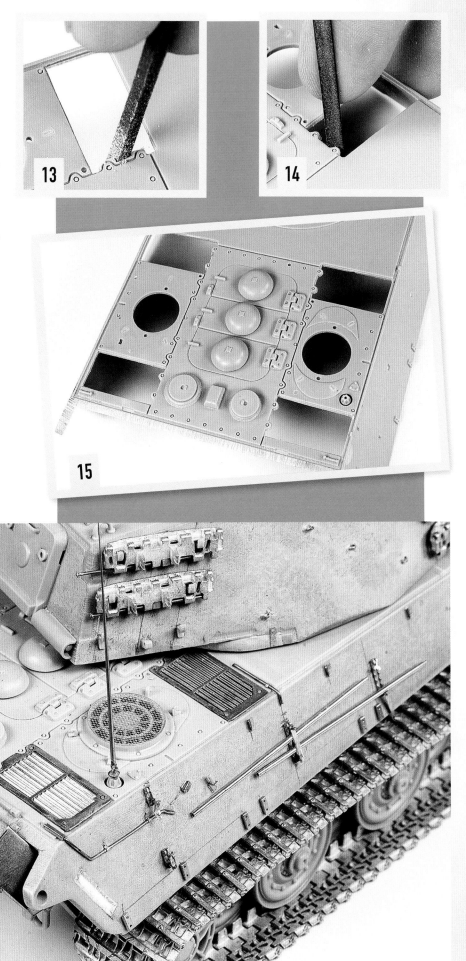

CLADDING LARGE OPEN AREAS

01

THERE ARE THOSE OCCASIONS DURING MODELLING A VEHICLE WHEN WE NEED TO COVER LARGE OPEN AREAS.

A great example are the sponsons on the under sides of the hulls over the top runs of track missing on the older Tamiya kits. I think that most veteran modellers have a King Tiger or something similar that has been sitting in the display case for the past decade or two. You know the one where you can look down through the hatches and see the upper sections of the tracks. To solve this problem one can simply glue the hatches closed but many modellers prefer to include figures in their vehicles. I personally like leaving the hatches open even without figures in order to add a bit life to the finished subject.

The Tamiya JS-3 model used in this book is now over ten years old. Its major drawback once assembled like most other Tamiya models from the 70s and 80s are the large open areas on the lower hull over the tracks. These areas needed to be filled in order to obtain the final appearance that I had envisioned on the finished project. In this part I will show some techniques that you can use to close large unwanted open sections like these.

PHOTO 1:
When viewing the rear photo of this JS-3 one can clearly see the inverted slopped armour normally hidden by the running gear and sheet metal structures located on both sides of the vehicle. I was captivated when I first became aware of this rather radical design and immediately knew that I wanted to display one of the sides uncovered. To do this I decided to have one of the sheet metal assemblies ripped away in order to expose the inverted slopped plate while also completely changing the appearance on one side of this very popular subject.

I also decided to remove the sheet metal structure on the opposite side as you saw in the last chapter. I wanted to replace it with more authentic looking parts rebuilt from copper sheet allowing for easier placement of realistic battle damage. We will look at how this side was reconstructed later.

02

PHOTO 2 AND 3:
The first thing that I needed to do was rebuild the plate thicknesses, weld detail and flame cut edges for the lower side and upper slopped front plates. Most of the techniques needed to perform these tasks have been or will be discussed in this book.

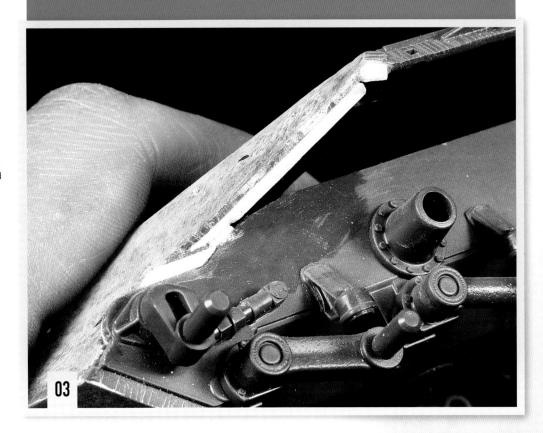

03

PHOTO 4 THROUGH 8:

I found an spare, thick ridged piece of sheet plastic, placed it against the hull, and traced the boundaries of the opening obtaining a rough idea of the shapes needed to fill these areas. The back side of my hobby knife with the aid of a straight edge was used to quickly cut the parts from the plastic. I used a flat sander to remove the bevels caused by the back edge of the knife. Notches needed to be added with a file in order to fit the piece around details located on the hulls interior.

PHOTO 9 AND 10:

As I demonstrated earlier, super glue and accelerator works great when quickly assembling large parts. Once the plastic was firmly located liquid cement was brushed into all of the seams in order to obtain a stronger bond. Liquid plastic cement usually does not interfere with the super glued areas.

PHOTO 11 AND 12:

After the liquid glue had an evening to set I started cladding the larger gaps with pieces of thin plastic strip. Super glue and accelerator where used to quickly secure the plastic strips while also filling the remaining seams. After giving the glue five to ten minutes to dry I cut the excess pieces of the sheet plastic away then sanded everything smooth.

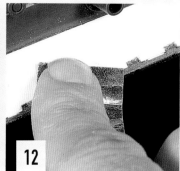

PHOTO 13 THROUGH 15:

After the super glued seams were polished flat I then added some putty over these areas and again sanded it smooth. The putty helped to ensure that no remaining seams would be visible through the paint.

You can see that the large seam where the lower hull side and inverted plate met was not filled at this time. The two parts in this area were joined by a large weld seam. In the next segment we will continue working on the hull of this JS-III by discussing different methods of simulating weld detail.

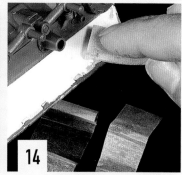

01

WHEN YOU START DETAILING OR CONVERTING SCALE MODELS YOU WILL ALSO RUN IN TO INSTANCES WHERE YOU NEED TO ADD OR REPLACE WELD SEAMS

Weld beads can differ in texture depending on the type of process used to apply them and the thickness of the steel plates they are bonding. The textures of weld beads also can differ on armoured fighting vehicles from various nations and even different factories within the same countries. Although not always the case I have observed that weld beads on AFVs produced in wartime Germany, for example, are often to a higher standard than weld beads produced on Soviet vehicles during the same period.

On these small replicas it can be sometimes difficult to tell the difference from one type of texture to the other once the vehicle is assembled. But the textures of welds bonding larger details such as some of the thicker hull and turret plates used on heavy armour can be noticeable and rather important.

PHOTO 1 AND 2:
 Let's look at a few examples of actual welds before we move forward. Again, welds come in many different textures. The fillet and groove welds seen on this Charioteer Mk VII in the first two photos are rather sound. In fact, good weld beads are more difficult to reproduce because the smooth edges and face can be a bit time-consuming to replicate.

02

03

PHOTO 3 AND 4:

The large fillet and smaller multiple pass welds on the lower hull of this King Tiger, although a bit rougher then the first examples, are still sound. I usually recreate these types of welds using a two-part epoxy.

Photo four shows a smaller mutable pass fillet weld on the turret of a Soviet JS-II. Although plenty sufficient for its task note that this weld has multiple irregularities such as undercut and overlap. These weld beads are the easiest examples to duplicate on scale models because

of the simple fact that they are not perfect. These types of welds can be fabricated simply using stretched sprue, a hobby knife and liquid cement as I will now demonstrate.

04

REPLICATING WELDS FROM STRETCHED SPRUE

YOU CAN CREATE CONVINCING LOOKING WELDS RATHER QUICKLY USING STRETCHED SPRUE.

I decided to use stretched sprue to make the large weld seam mating the lower and upper inverted hull plates on the JS-3. I knew this weld would be rather hidden once the model was finished and the running gear attached so I did not want to devote too much time creating it. Let's look at how to make a weld seam using stretched sprue.

>> **PHOTO 1 THROUGH 3:**
To start I found a length of sprue without any part numbers or details and cut it from the rest of the frame. I warmed it on center using a lighter and slowly pulled it apart. Next I cut the length to size and laid it over the groove on the model where I wanted to add some weld detail. I brushed some liquid cement over the sprue and let it set for about five minutes.

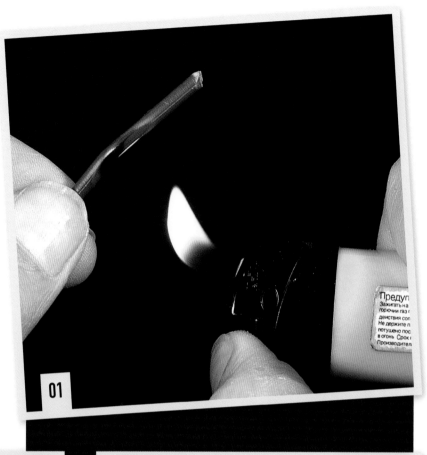

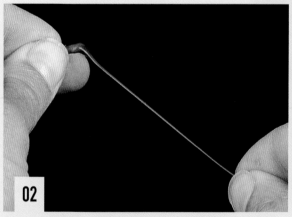

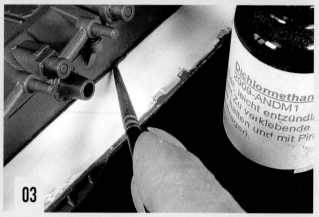

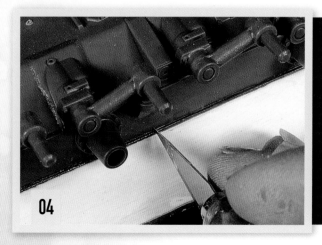

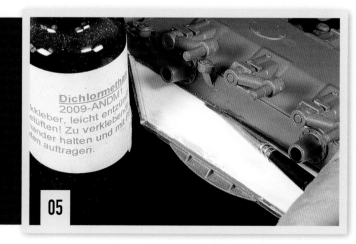

06

07

PHOTO 4 THROUGH 7:

Once the liquid cement had softened the sprue I started texturing it using a new sharp hobby blade working from one end toward the other. Once you have textured the entire weld bead add more liquid glue over the entire length and then repeat the process. On larger weld beads such as this you might need to repeat the process of adding glue and texturing four to five times to obtain a convincing texture. Always finish the procedure by adding a final coat of liquid cement over the bead.

Stretched sprue is an easy way to create basic looking weld beads. As I showed you at the beginning of this segment, larger weld beads seen on AFVs can vary and different methods are needed to recreate them. Next we will recreate some larger sounder welds using a two-part epoxy.

The weld around the perimeter of this BT-7A was created using stretched sprue and liquid cement textured using a hobby knife.

IMITATING WELDS USING A TWO-PART EPOXY
IN THE LAST SECTION I DEMONSTRATED HOW TO EASILY CREATE BASIC WELDS USING SPRUE AND LIQUID CEMENT.

These mediums are great for smaller welds or those created for applications representing lower quality standards.

Two-part epoxies are also very good for creating larger sound welds with limited irregularities often observed bonding thicker plates of steel. In this instance we are going to place a groove weld on the outer perimeter of this Tiger I turret.

 PHOTO 1:
Apoxie Sculpt is a two-part compound that works well for everything from sculpting figures to building up surfaces and creating tarps. Here we will use it to create realistic weld seams. You will also need a sculpting tool or toothpick, a glass of water and a short length of small diameter tubing.

 PHOTO 2 THROUGH 5:
The first thing you need to do is take a small ball from each part of the Epoxy and press them together until they are thoroughly mixed. Once the components are mixed, roll a thin length as in photo five. You will have about 20 minutes to work with the mixed components until they start to solidify.

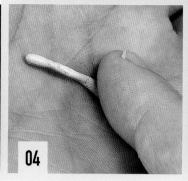

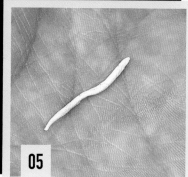

PHOTO 6 THROUGH 8:

Cut the tapered edges from the length and place it into location. In this case a toothpick dampened with water was used to press the length of epoxy into location. Simply use your finger, also dampened with water, to smooth the putty preparing it for texturing.

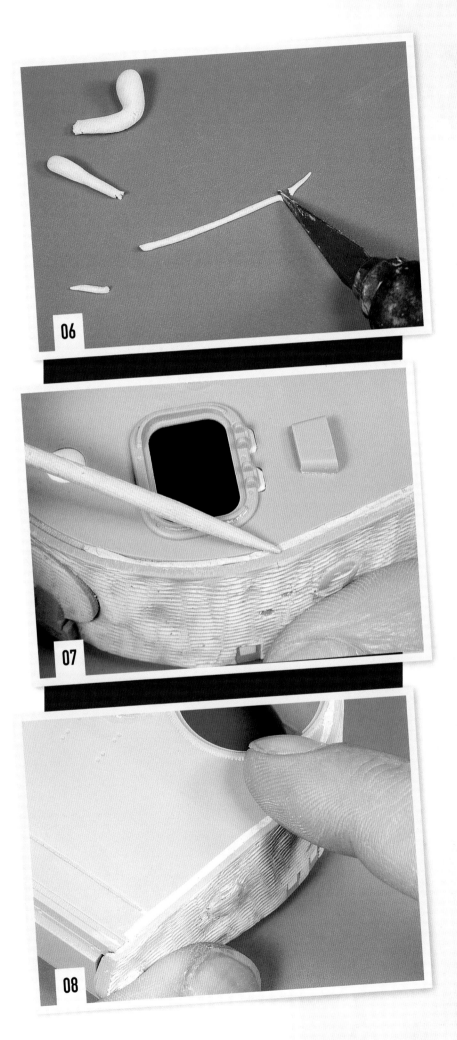

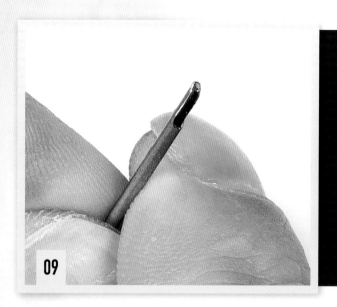

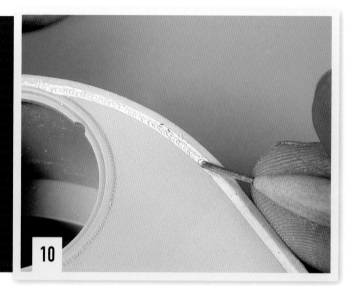

PHOTO 9 AND 10:

The tool in photo nine was made from a small diameter length of brass tubing. The notch and bevel at the end where created carefully using a small grinder attached to a rotary tool. Once I removed the burrs from the tooled brass tube it was glued into a wooden handle. Using a very light taping motion I started texturing the weld seam as shown in photo ten. Dip the brass tool into water in order to keep the putty from sticking to it during texturing.

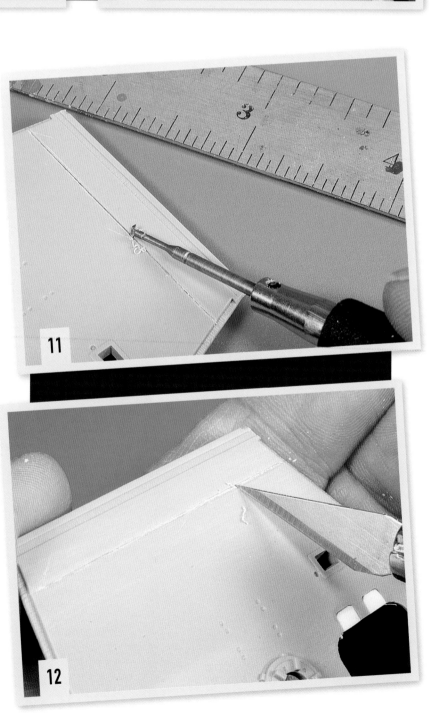

PHOTO 11 AND 12:

Sometimes you will need to create a groove when applying weld seams on a flat surface. For the groove weld running across the top of the turret I engraved a notch using a panel scriber and straight edge. Panel scribers are used more commonly by aircraft modellers. They are great to have in your tool box for applications such as this. Panel scribers like this one come with mutable ends for a variety of applications. To finish the groove I beveled each side by carefully running the edge of a hobby-knife down each length as shown in photo 12. Again, I created the weld seam using a two-part epoxy and then textured it as I did with the weld around the outer edge of the turret.

Although a little more skill and time is needed to create welds using two-part epoxies the final appearance is far more authentic. Apoxie Sculpt is great for a number of uses. One of the more common applications that armour modellers use it for is creating zimmerit patterns as we'll discus next.

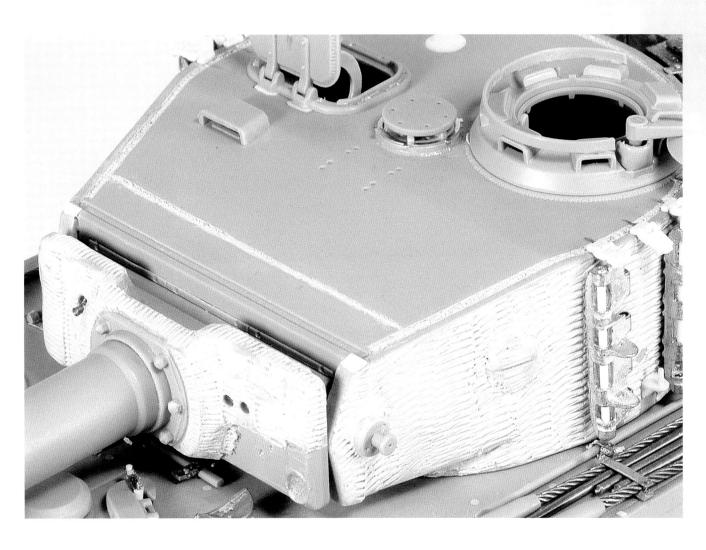

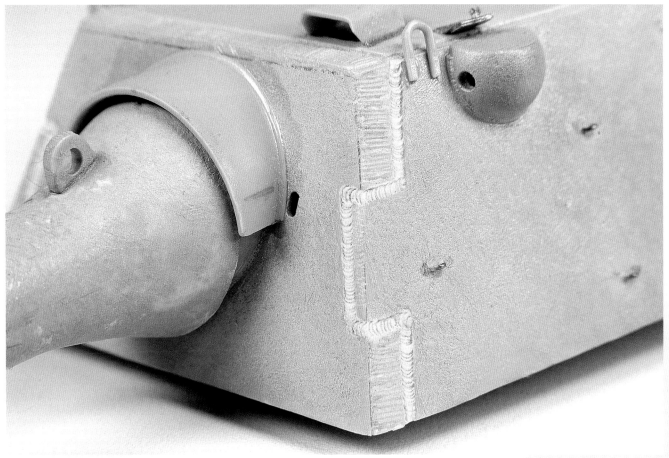

08

ZIMMERIT

ONE OF THE UNIQUE FEATURES OF GERMAN AFVS IS THE APPLICATION OF A NON-MAGNETIC COATING APPLIED DURING 1943 TO 1944 REFERRED TO AS ZIMMERIT.

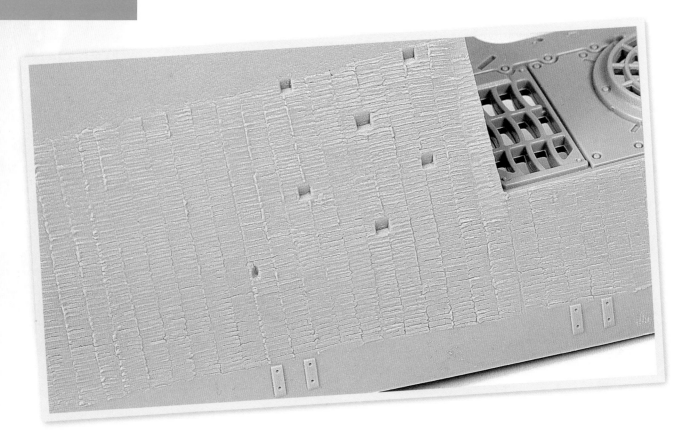

This coating was invented to protect German AFVs from magnetically attached anti-tank-mines. The idea was to provide a non-ferrous coat over the armour plating that would inhibit these explosives from sticking to the vehicle. Replicating authentic zimmerit patterns onto scale models can be a bit tricky and stressful for a number of reasons. These fine, sometimes very random, patterns can be difficult to properly produce to scale. There are a number of two-part epoxies and putties available and one must choose a type in which you feel most comfortable using. I will demonstrate a few kinds that I have experience with momentarily. There are also after market companies such as Atak and Cavalier which offer very fine cast resin sheets of pretty authentic-looking Zimmerit that you can glue to the sides of a model. These sets also require some simple additional techniques that will also be discussed.

Luckily, today hi-end injection moulded kits are available with zimmerit patterns moulded into the plastic parts which do not actually look too bad. The drawbacks to these kits are that it can be difficult to create authentic damage to the zimmerit coats such as flaking along with other areas which have been broken away due to impacts for example. There has also been some

controversy about the patterns in the first releases of these injection moulded kits being unrealistically even. The pattern on this Jagdtiger above from DML is rather nice. Before we get started with some examples of zimmerit, lets first take a brief look at the history of this anti magnetic paste.

Zimmerit was first developed by the German company Chemische Werke Zimmer AG, hence the name Zimmerit, but records indicate that this was produced by other manufacturers, possibly even factories, because of the huge demand. A Tiger I for example needed 200kg of the paste to cover the appropriate areas of the hull and turret. Zimmerit paste contained the following components: barium sulfate (40%), polyvinyl acetate (25%), ochre pigment for the dark yellow colour (15%), Zinc sulfide (10%) and wood fiber (10%).

Despite the fact that the official order was given on December 29th 1943, the application of Zimmerit onto AFVs started much earlier. Sources state that, for example, the application of Zimmerit on Tiger I tanks commenced from mid-August 1943 in the factories. Starting from October 1943 all newly produced tanks and assault guns received their coating on the

assembly line. These tanks in question which had already been delivered to the front lines were ordered to receive the application in the field. In general zimmerit was applied to tanks used in front line service starting from the Panzer III and IV, Tigers, Panthers and Assault Guns, like the StuG III and IV or the Elefant. Vehicles which weren't intended for front line service, including self propelled artillery, usually had no zimmerit application. Despite the order only a few examples were retrofitted with zimmerit at the frontlines.

In August 1944 rumours arose that the zimmerit coating would easily catch fire when the tank was hit. The Generalinspekteur der Panzertruppen (High Command of the Armed Forces) ceased the application of zimmerit on September 9th 1944. The official order followed one month later. Even though the initial assumption proved to be wrong it can be assumed that there were also other reasons for this decision. Zimmerit increased the weight of the vehicle resulting in higher fuel consumption. Its application also increased manufacturing lead times and after all, the Germans were the only army at the time using magnetic mines against tanks in a large scale. Let's now look at the more common zimmerit patterns.

ZIMMERIT PATTERNS

EVEN THOUGH PRECISE ORDERS WERE GIVEN ON HOW AND WHERE TO APPLY ZIMMERIT THE FACTORIES SOON DEVELOPED THEIR OWN VARIOUS PATTERNS RESULTING IN ABOUT A DOZEN DIFFERENT TYPES.

The most common pattern was the one with vertical columns of horizontal ridges but there were also patterns composed of small squares or the distinctive "waffle" pattern applied onto StuG IIIs at the Alkett plant.

The zimmerit paste was applied directly onto the primed surface of the vehicle. It was ordered to apply the paste in two coats using a trowel. The first coat was to be 5mm thick and marked out in squares using the edge of the trowel. This coat had to be heated with a blow torch in order to remove the solvent ensuring that it would firmly adhere onto the vehicle. After this treatment the coat had to dry for another 24 hours. The second coat applied was thinner and marked in lines with a metal comb. The produced pattern improved the adhesion of this second coat and resulted in a very rough and uneven surface that would be difficult for magnetic mines to stick to. However there have been variations during the application as mentioned before. The methods and the tools used during the fabrication obviously differ and have remained subject to discussion even until today. Here are some of the more common patterns.

>> PHOTO 1 THROUGH 3:
These first three examples contain the more commonly seen zimmerit pattern containing repeating columns of horizontal ridges. Note how this pattern has an irregular radius on the front of the Panzer IV turret around the mantlet. This Tiger II contains another example of this pattern. Note the very random crossing vertical columns. You can also see on the Tiger I that the columns of horizontal ridges are wider and larger on the turret then on the hull. This was normal in zimmerit patterns seen on Tiger I Tanks.

01

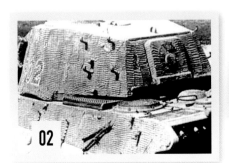

02

03

PHOTO 4 THROUGH 6:
The next three examples all have a zimmerit pattern with horizontal columns of vertical edges.

The panzer IV in photo five contains this pattern on the turret schürzen while the hull has the columns of horizontal ridges seen on the prior three examples. You can see on the second panzer IV that the vertical edges are spread further apart within the slightly wavy horizontal columns. This example again demonstrates that zimmerit patterns can be rather uneven. Remember that these patterns were applied by hand.

04

05

06

PHOTO 7:
This Panther G has a rather even intricate pattern typically seen on the ones produced at MAN of horizontal columns of vertical edges with a diagonal grooves.

PHOTO 8:
This photo shows another Panther this time an Ausf. A. This vehicle contains a zimmerit pattern having horizontal columns of vertical edges separated into relatively even squares by vertical grooves. Again you can see that the horizontal columns are slightly uneven.

PHOTO 9:
The rather rare zimmerit pattern on this Panzer IV consists of fine squares that are sometimes uneven as seen to the right of the covered hull machine gun.

10

PHOTO 10 AND 11:
These two StuG III Ausf G self-propelled guns both contain the unique "waffle" pattern applied at the Alkett-plant. On the first StuG you can see the uneven thickness of the pattern over the front hull plate. The zimmerit on the second vehicle contains some areas where the coat has flaked away. Again areas of uneven patterns can be seen in on both examples. You will also notice that these uneven areas are usually over the smaller plates and in between details where the required texture, as a result of a stamp being too large to fit between the details, would have been difficult to reproduce. As modellers we face this same problem on a smaller scale when creating zimmerit patterns on our replicas.

11

PHOTO 12:
The StuG III Ausf G in this photo appears to have a zimmerit pattern with repeating columns of horizontal ridges. This pattern also has parallel grooves separating the columns into small rectangles.

12

PHOTO 13 THROUGH 15:
These three Panther tanks all contain a square zimmerit pattern of rather evenly spaced horizontal and vertical grooves. Note the wandering of the grooves creating uneven patterns in certain areas particularly on the Panthers in photos 13 and 14.

13

14

15

PHOTO 16 AND 17:
Here are a few odd examples of zimmerit patterns. This Panzer IV contains a rough pattern over the turret schürzen and parts of the hull. This pattern was most likely applied in the field. This StuG III also has a distinct pattern of random ridges broken up by horizontally and vertical grooves.

These photos display some, but not all, of the different zimmerit patterns seen on German armour during the Second World War. You can see in these photos that most of these examples can be rather uneven in areas and also vary in thickness. I think that these differences will add more character when recreating zimmerit patterns on scale models. With a better

understanding of the different patterns, and the irregularities they can often contain, we can move on to some examples of applying zimmerit onto our models. I think that you will find zimmerit application rather enjoyable.

16

17

REPLICATING ZIMMERIT USING TWO-PART EPOXY

01

I HAVE FOUND THAT THE MOST CONVINCING RESULTS WHEN REPLICATING ZIMMERIT CAN BE OBTAINED USING TWO-PART EPOXIES AND POLYESTER PUTTIES

Although more time and patience is needed I prefer these mediums to after-market sets and injection moulded zimmerit because they give you the most flexibility when creating random patterns, flakes, and other damage caused by impacts for example.

In this segment I will provide you with some examples of zimmerit application using some different two-part putties that I have experience with. I will also apply a zimmerit pattern onto PE details demonstrating that putties can be applied onto this material using the same techniques. I will also be using both store-purchased and homemade tools to show examples on how to quickly obtain accurate results. Let's now move forward onto a Tiger I turret starting with Apoxie Sculpt.

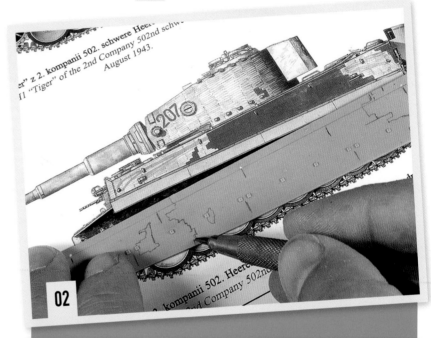

02

>> **PHOTO 1 THROUGH 3:**
Although the zimmerit pattern on the hull of this Tiger was simpler than the one on the turret it was finer and contains a lot of flaking and damage. Again, I only had one partial photo of the Tiger that this replica was modelled after, therefore I decided to reference the artist's interpretation that I had of the vehicle assuming that the illustrator knew more than I did.

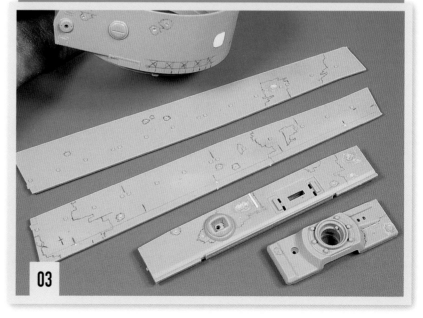

03

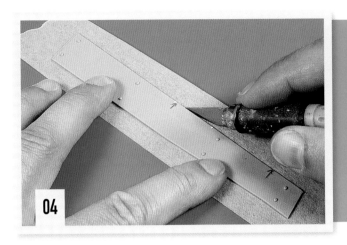

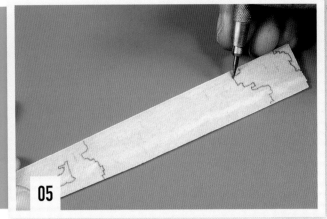

PHOTO 4 AND 5:
After sticking thin semi-transparent masking tape onto the outer sides of the parts, I cut it to size, than traced the pattern onto the adhesive.

PHOTO 6 AND 7:
I carefully cut out the traced pattern using my hobby knife then removed the unwanted sections. A bit of imagination was needed to cut the area around the circular MG mount on the front of the hull.

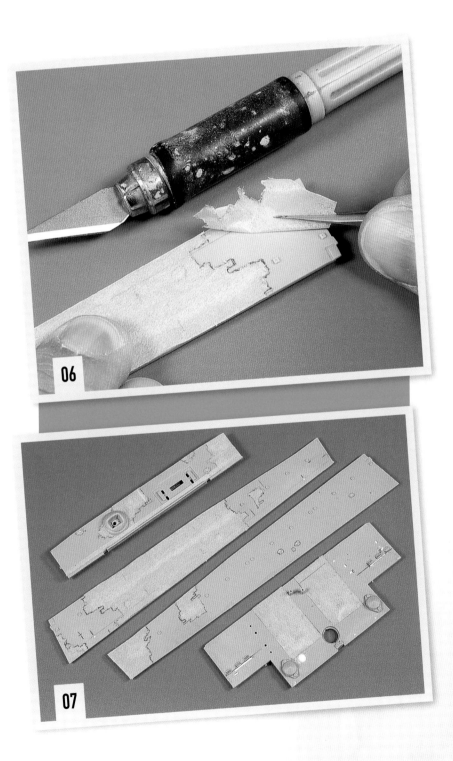

PHOTO 8:
Apoxie Sculpt is very popular with modellers for creating zimmerit patterns. It has a slow drying time allowing plenty of time to obtain a pattern that you are happy with. It will start to solidify becoming more difficult to manipulate in about 20 minutes.

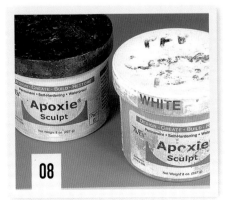

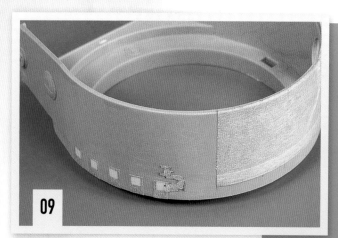

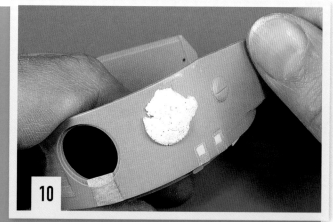

PHOTO 9 THROUGH 11:

Masking tape was used to cover all of the areas that I would want free of zimmerit. It is best to break your model into imaginary pieces and applying the zimmerit pattern onto each one at a time. In this case I broke the turret into right and left hand sides. After mixing small amounts of the two-part putty I started applying balls onto the right hand side of the turret than spreading them over the surface using my finger with the aid of water. Apoxie Sculpt tends to be a bit hard so patience is needed insuring that it is evenly spread over surface of the model to a scaled thickness.

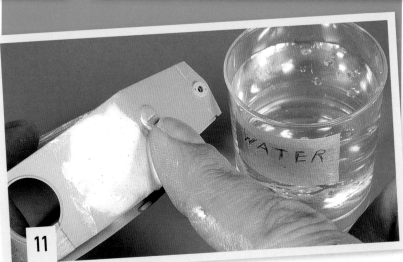

PHOTO 12 THROUGH 14:

Rolling thin cylindrical objects like Toothpicks over the putty will also help you to spread it over the surface of the plastic and around details. Remember to take your time making sure that the putty is evenly distributed thinly across the entire surface before applying the pattern. Use your hobby knife to clear any excess putty away from the corners.

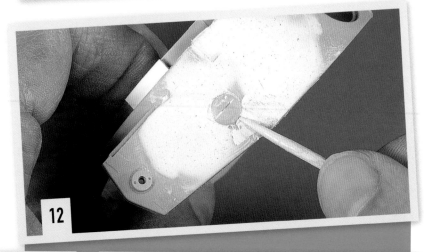

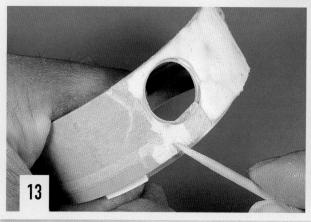

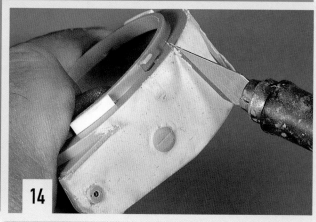

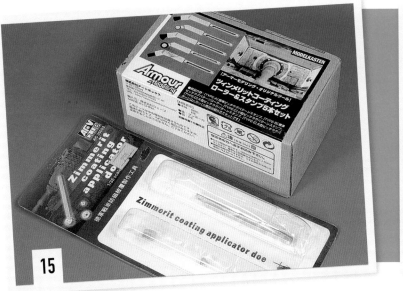

PHOTO 15 AND 16:
There are numerous roller-type tools available to aid in making patterns. The two examples in photo 15 were the ones I had on hand and they both work well. The pattern on the turret was different than that seen on the side of the hull. The pattern on the turret and hull in photo 16 are identical to the one reference photo that I had in hand of the Tiger I that this model represents.

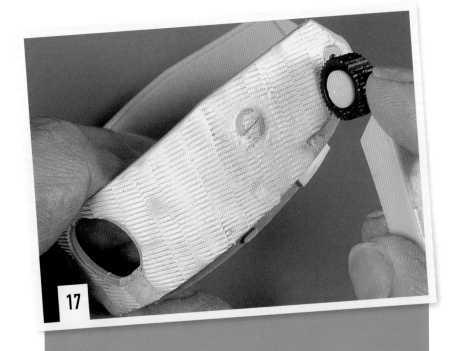

PHOTO 17 AND 18:
Immediately after spreading the putty to an even thickness, I lightly rolled the tool over it. To obtain this particular pattern I started by first rolling the tool downward in a slightly diagonal pattern in rows moving from one side of the turret to the other. I finished by going over the first pattern with a vertical motion again starting from one side and working in side by side in rows to the opposite end.

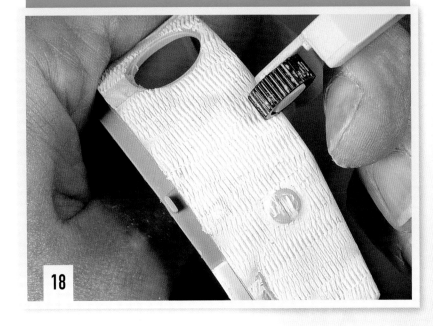

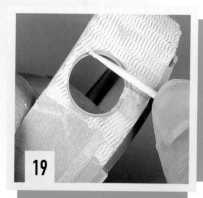

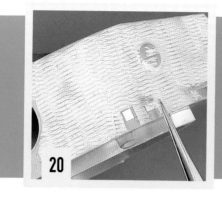

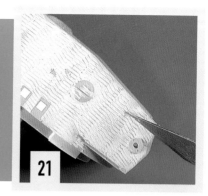

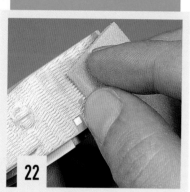

PHOTO 19 THROUGH 22:
A toothpick was used to remove any unwanted putty from difficult to reach areas. All of the tape used to mask areas from the putty was also peeled away. Damage in the pattern caused by fragments were also added using a hobby knife prior to the putty solidifying. Once hardened I lightly polished the zimmerit pattern using fine sandpaper.

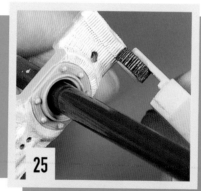

PHOTO 23 THROUGH 27:
The mantlet required a little more time and skill due to its slightly more complex shape. I slid the mantlet onto a tapered brush handle to firmly hold the part without ruining the soft zimmerit pattern. This time, after evenly spreading the putty over the part, I created the pattern in the recessed areas using a piece of plastic card cut to the proper width and sharpened at one end. I used the roller to finish the pattern and removed the masking tape.

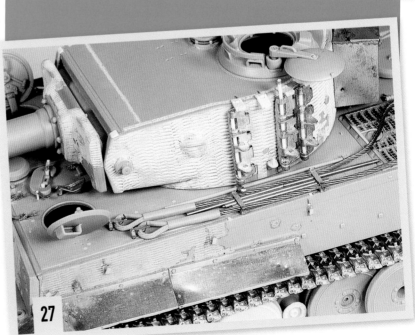

PHOTO 28 THROUGH 30:

Although the zimmerit pattern on the hull of this Tiger I was simpler than the one on the turret it was finer as usually seen on this AFV. Mori Mori putty is another option. This product from Japan is a very fine polyester putty. It will start to solidify within minutes after you mix it with just a bit of the hardener. What I mean by a 'bit' is about 50% putty to around 1% hardener. Mori Mori putty is extremely easy to spread over the part allowing you to create a pattern that is very close to scale. The problem is that it solidifies quickly and you need to be much faster when creating your zimmerit pattern. I applied the Mori Mori putty using all of the same techniques applied to the Apoxie Sculpt while creating the pattern on the turret. As on the turret I removed the masking tape once the zimmerit pattern was applied and before it could dry.

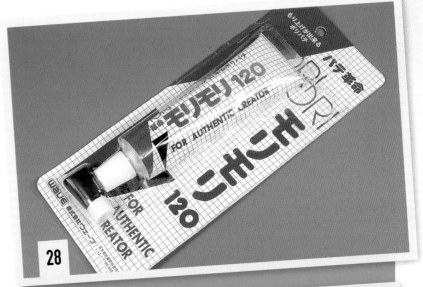

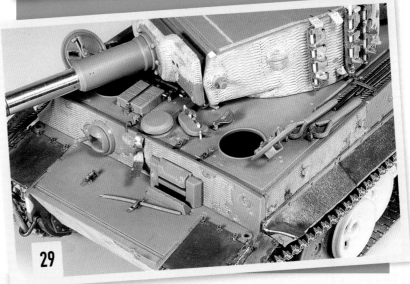

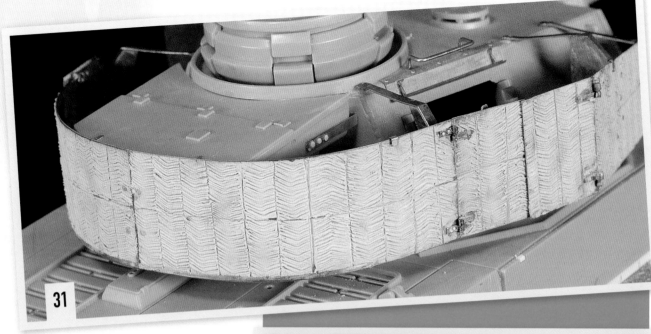

PHOTO 31 AND 32:

Let's move onto another example of a more complex zimmerit pattern containing vertical columns of diagonal ridges located on the turret Schürzen of this Pazer IV H in the 4.Panzer-Division on the Eastern Front during 1944. You can apply polyester putties onto photo etched parts pretty much as easily as you can on plastic. Prior to starting I made my own tools from sections of copper sheet formed using a bending tool. For this example I decided to use anther polyester putty offered by Tamiya.

PHOTO 33 THROUGH 35:

A bit thicker than the Mori Mori, the Tamiya putty will start to solidify within five to ten minutes after you mix it with the hardener. The ratio of putty and hardener is about the same as with the Mori Mori type. You can use a bit of water to thin the mixture making it easier to apply if you feel it necessary.

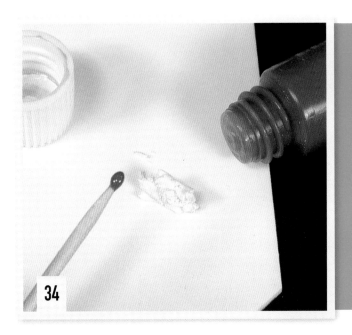

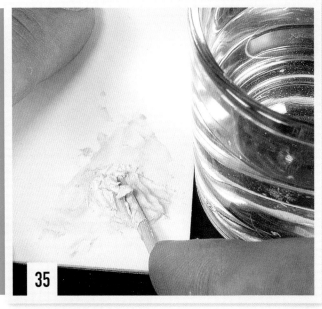

PHOTO 36 THROUGH 39:
After carefully studying reference photos I applied the pattern onto the first side of the Schürzen and let it solidify overnight prior to moving onto the second side. Again, polyester putties solidify quickly so it is better to break the subject down into sections applying and forming the zimmerit pattern in one area at a time. Application of a zimmerit pattern using Tamiya putty was much the same as when using the Apoxie Sculpt. Like with the mantlet, I applied the putty first in small amounts and started to spread it using a toothpick. I finished distributing it evenly over the surface using my finger dampened with water. The toothpick was used to clean unwanted putty off of the fine details.

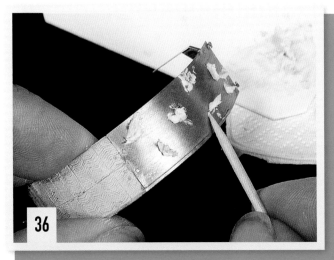

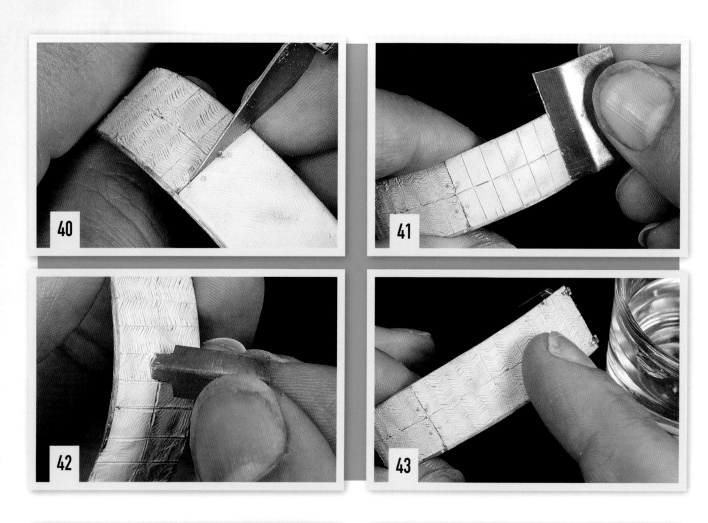

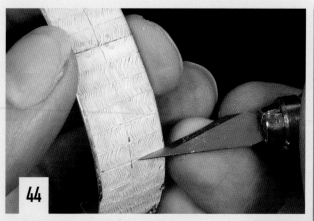

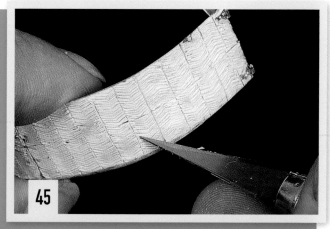

PHOTO 40 THROUGH 43:
Next the vertical lines where made using both my knife and my custom made copper zimmerit tool. Dampen the tools with tap water to keep the putty from sticking to them. After I pressed the diagonal parts of the pattern I gently rubbed the entire pattern with my finger dampened with water.

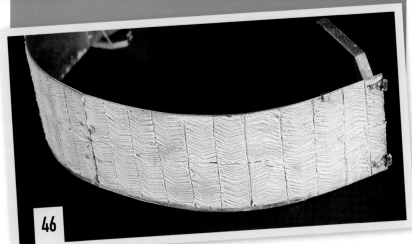

PHOTO 44 THROUGH 48:
I needed to carefully touch up some of the areas on the pattern using my hobby knife where I pressed it hard when smoothing it. I allowed the putty to dry overnight.

If you are patient, self-made zimmerit using two-part putties gives you the most authentic looking zimmerit patterns. There are plenty of after-market zimmerit kits that also look rather good and are designed to fit specific models.

The techniques needed to apply some of these sets are rather easy. Next we will look at a few things to remember when applying a resin cast after-market zimmerit kit to a model.

47

48

WORKING WITH AFTER-MARKET RESIN ZIMMERIT

IN THIS SEGMENT I WOULD LIKE TO TALK A LITTLE ABOUT THE APPLICATION OF RESIN ZIMMERIT.

The two more popular brands that have been producing these aftermarket sets are Atak and Cavalier. Although I have read minor complaints about cast resin zimmerit sets sometimes shrinkage can be a problem, synonymous with resin, the majority of the users appear to be happy with them.

PHOTO 1 AND 2:
We will look at examples of Atak zimmerit sets. One of them was for the Dragon models Tiger P kit and the other for the King Tiger mounting the Porsche Turret from the same brand. The resin casting on the parts in both of the sets was really good. The zimmerit patterns looked fine, crisp and also random where it should be.

PHOTO 3 AND 4:
The larger sections of zimmerit that covered the hull were cast in very fine sheets. Although close to scale, you probably will have one chance to properly locate and attach these thin pieces onto the hull. The best way to remove these details from the sheets is with a new sharp hobby blade. You can also see that the whole upper part of the zimmerit covered turret was included in the King Tiger kit. .

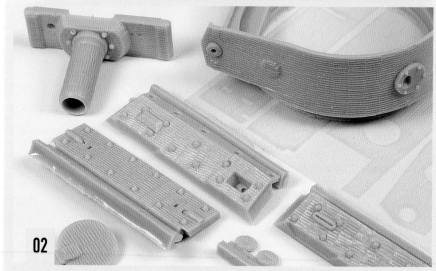

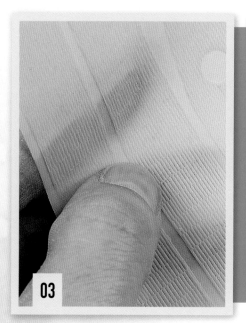

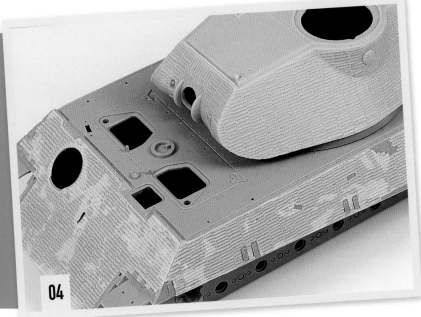

PHOTO 5 THROUGH 8:

The zimmerit set used on the Jagdpanther was also from Atak (ref no. 35043) and without any casting flaws. This model represents the Jagdpanther no. 112 seen on pages 512 and 514 of the book, "The Combat History of the Schwere Panzer Abteilung 654" by Karlheinz Munch. These Jagdpanthers had some field modifications mostly consisting of the relocation of exterior components and tools.

The small impacts seen in the zimmerit were added once the sections were removed from the resin sheets. After carefully gluing the sheets onto the model, Tamiya modelling putty thinned with liquid cement was used to seal any gaps between the kit superstructure and the thin layer of resin zimmerit. Some small sections of the zimmerit needed to be removed with a fine grinding bit and rotary tool for the relocation of components such as this fire extinguisher. Note the other exterior resin components, also offered by Atak (ref no. 35A08), used to backdate the Tamiya model.

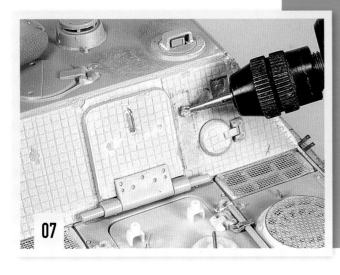

09

10

PHOTO 9 THROUGH 12:
A two-part epoxy putty and techniques described earlier were used to create the zimmerit pattern around the corners of the hull and superstructure and also over the front fender and rear tool box. A hobby knife was needed to remove some of the squares giving the layer of zimmerit an authentic chipped appearance.

You can see how the rough texture of the zimmerit can be better observed after all of the painting techniques have been applied to the finished model.

11

12

ALONG WITH DAMAGE AND AUTHENTIC WEATHERING APPLYING IMPACTS CAN REALLY HELP TO ADD BOTH LIFE AND CHARACTER TO A COMPLETED ARMOUR MODEL.

Impacts are fun to create and can even allow you to present various details in a different manner such as the busted track link on the side of this Tiger II/E-75 turret below.

PHOTO 1 THROUGH 3:

Impacts vary in both size and appearance. Here are a few different examples for reference. This unfortunate Panther G shows three penetrating rounds that appear to have hit directly into the side of the turret. This KV-1 at the Parola Museum in Finland shows an impact that hit at a sharp angle on the hull front. This BT-7 M42, also at the Parola Museum, has impacts in the front of the hull from small arms fire. These impacts were probably created when the vehicle was manufactured to test the quality of the steel. They are a good example of smaller impacts and should also be present on veteran AFVs.

The Tiger I seen throughout out this book has a number of various sized impacts that I created on different parts. I wanted to depict a Tiger-I still in operation therefore I wanted none of the impacts to have completely penetrated. Let's start with the blows that this veteran took on the larger plates.

PHOTO 4:
If you want to create multiple impacts I cannot stress enough the importance of randomness. Start by studying photos of the AFVs or similar types of vehicles to the one you are modelling. Look through books and on the web to obtain an idea of where you would like to place each of the hits. After reviewing impacts in photos of different Tiger Is I drew the blows onto the model using a pencil. This way I could simply erase and relocate the hits if I was not happy with the arrangement.

PHOTO 5 AND 6:
For the larger impacts I simply filed a flat edge onto the end of my soldering iron. The smaller impacts also seen in this photo were created with the same iron but using a pointier tip.

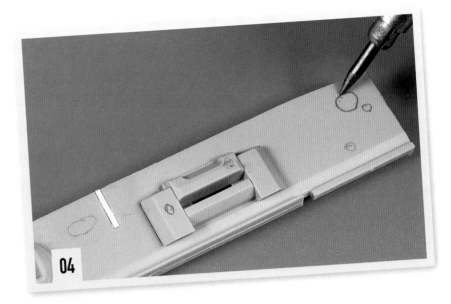

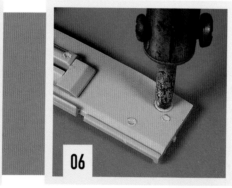

PHOTO 7 THROUGH 9:
After creating the indents some of the excess plastic was carefully removed using a hobby knife. Liquid cement and putty were used to soften any sharp edges left from the knife while adding a slight hint of texture. An old hobby blade warmed using a cigarette lighter was used to add small dings caused by the numerous fragments that ripped away from the impact. These little fragment impacts are often missed.

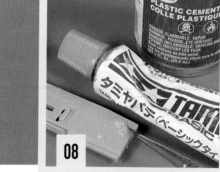

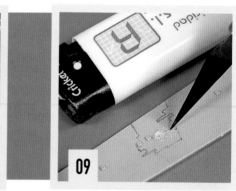

PHOTO 10:
It is important that you consider how some of the smaller details around impacts might be affected. Note the broken shovel and damaged light mount. Again, impacts are a good means for allowing you to be creative in presenting details differently.

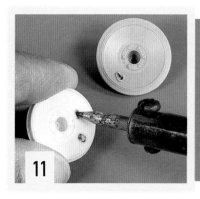

PHOTO 11 AND 12:
The impacts that penetrated the thinner wheels were approached a bit differently. The road wheels where made from a lighter guage steel. Once more, I made the penetrations using a hot pointed soldering iron. I ground away some of the plastic on the opposite side of the penetrations making the thickness of the wheel appear more to scale when viewed from the opposite side where it will be visible.

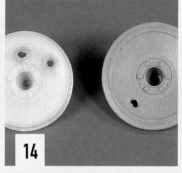

PHOTO 13 THROUGH 16:
As before liquid glue and putty were used to smooth any sharp edges that look like knife marks. Resin parts are much like plastic when worked with in this manner. The small arms impacts in the photo-etched turret basket will also be discussed. Next we will discuss techniques for working with photo-etched brass.

.

10 WORKING WITH PHOTO ETCH & OTHER METALLIC PARTS

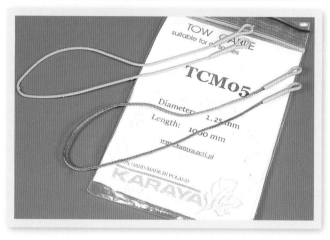

PHOTO-ETCHED BRASS (PE) HAS BEEN A GREAT RESOURCE AVAILABLE FOR OVER 20 YEARS NOW ALLOWING MODELLERS TO ADD AUTHENTIC FINE DETAILS TO THEIR REPLICAS.

The different PE sets and accessories obtainable today offer a large selection of intricate parts and assemblies that are often too thin and detailed to produce in injection moulded plastic. Good photo etch skills will also allow modellers to have an extra dimension of creativity as I will demonstrate further on in this segment. Often separated into sub-assemblies such as fenders, grills and miscellaneous details there can sometimes be three to four sets available for one specific model. Most PE companies are now offering kits containing all of their sets for specific popular subjects in one package. These box sets are often handy as you get everything you need enclosed. They can also be rather extensive even for experienced modellers sometimes requiring large amounts of time. PE companies also offer turned brass parts such as smoke discharges, radio antenna basses, ammunition shells and even sets of telephone poles for example. These details are also handy as they contain no seams and therefore no

cleaning is required. Other useful detailing mediums such as brass wire, tow cables, tubing and structural shapes are also available.

Most PE sets are relatively inexpensive but the problem with PE is that it requires skill, practice and can also be time consuming to both assemble and attach onto a model. PE is very delicate. These thin parts can be easily bent, broken away and lost both during and after assembly. Preparing a model for PE can also be difficult sometimes resulting in the destruction of a kit when replacing grills for example if the modeller is not experienced. Effectively assembling PE takes practice but is well worth using. It is best to assemble and prepare as much of the model as possible prior to adding any PE. This is why methods such as removing segments of plastic, cladding large open areas and applying zimmerit were discussed earlier in this book.

Applying the PE details for me is usually the last step prior to painting the model.

What I am going to demonstrate in the first section of this chapter are some examples using basic PE assemblies along with the tools, consumables, and methods that I employ when working with this medium. I will then demonstrate some more of these skills by putting together a rather complex assembly that requires many different parts to complete. In the final part of this chapter I will create some of my own parts and details from scratch using copper sheet, brass shapes and various PE details.

Before we start I would also like to mention that using PE to finish a replica is not always necessary. I would strongly recommend that beginners concentrate on becoming more efficient with the critical assembly fundamentals discussed earlier before moving onto using PE.

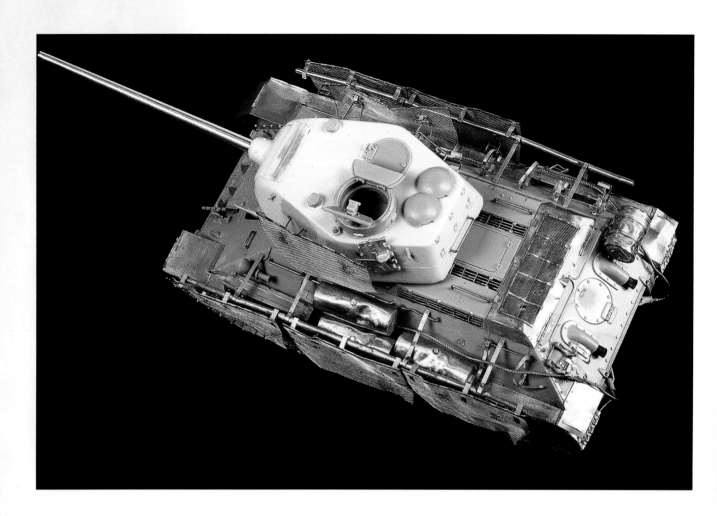

BASIC BRASS AND PHOTO ETCH ASSEMBLING TECHNIQUES

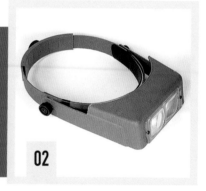

PHOTO 1 AND 2:
Most of the tools that I will be working with in these segments to assemble PE parts can be seen in photo one. A number of pliers and a bending tool will also be important. There are a number of bending tools on the market that all work fairly well. Make sure that you purchase a metal one that cannot be damaged during soldering. I also keep an Opti-visor handy for very fine parts.

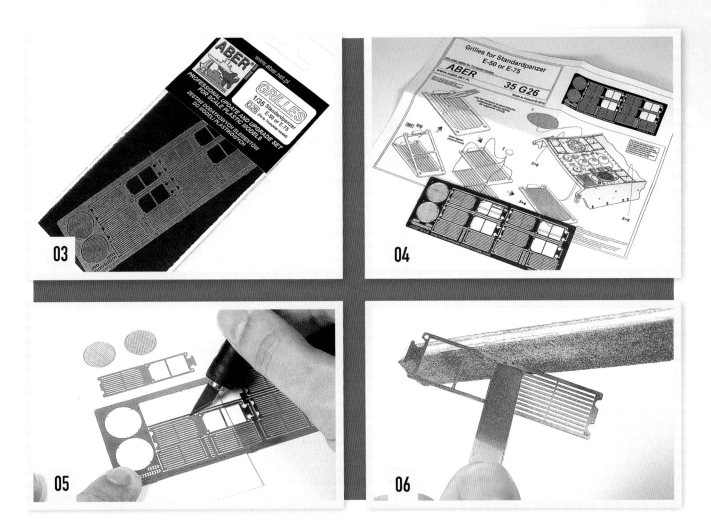

PHOTO 3 THROUGH 6:

Let's start with the methods needed to assemble these basic sets of E-50/75 louvers. These four details consisted of two major pieces and which one needed to be formed and soldered prior to assembly. It is easiest to cut the PE parts from the fret using a square piece of plastic and a number 24 X-acto blade. Clean the parts using a pair of flat pliers and sanding sticks.

PHOTO 7 THROUGH 9:

The flat surfaces and griping ability on a good set of flat pliers can make an efficient bending tool. It will be worth your time to visit a Jeweller's supply store and investing a bit extra on good stainless steel sets of pliers that will grip squarely while lasting you a lifetime. Flat pliers and a metal ruler are all that is needed to make nice fine bends.

Soldering is the method that I commonly use to assemble PE while only resorting to super glue when attaching small parts like bolts and rivets for example. Soldering a part creates a stronger cleaner bond than when using superglue. There

are many devices and methods available for soldering PE. Some of these items such as resistance soldering tools are rather costly. There are also heat devices such as hand held torches that I have been informed can work rather well.

I have always used a 40W 220-240 volt iron when soldering PE. One of these tools will cost you very little. The heat output of an iron like this is localized allowing you to even solder assemblies that are already glued onto the model without damaging the plastic if you are fast enough. I use a thin diameter soldering wire of around .015" when possible, always without a flux core.

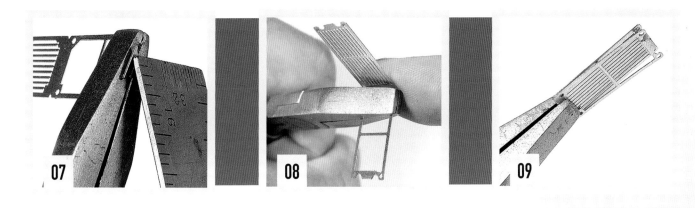

PHOTO 10 THROUGH 13:

Try to keep the iron as clean as possible while soldering. Employ an old file for this task because the flux used during soldering will cause it to rust over time. Also use an old brush to apply the liquid solder where the part is to be joined. Apply a bit of solder onto the end of the hot iron as shown. If the solder does not adhere to the iron you will need to adjust its heat and/or clean the end.

PHOTO 14 AND 15:

It can be easy to apply too much solder onto a part. You will know with experience when to remove some of the excess solder from the end of the iron before soldering the part. You can wipe the excess solder away from the hot iron onto a piece of metal such as this aluminum square prior to placing any onto the parts. To solder the pieces lightly touch the iron onto where the flux was applied. The flux will help the solder to flow into the groove by capillary action strongly bonding the part.

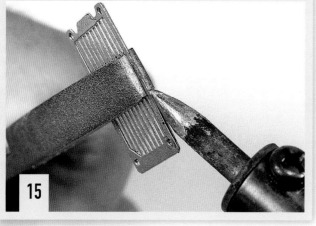

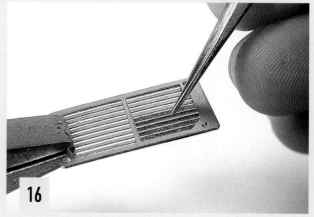

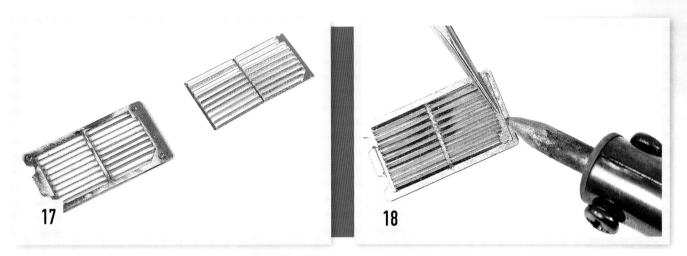

PHOTO 16 THROUGH 18:
After soldering the folded sets of louvers the parts were much stronger as a result of the two thicknesses. It would now be much easer to bend each of the louvers to the correct angle without causing any unwanted bends in the parts. After forming the louvers I assembled the two larger parts that made up each set.

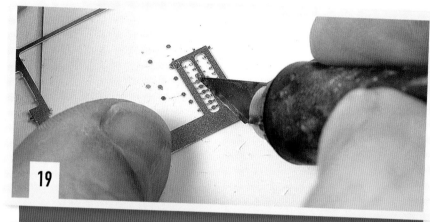

PHOTO 19 THROUGH 21:
I attached the bolts onto the louvers using superglue. Sometimes superglue dries much slower when used on metal parts. You will need to let pieces sit for around five to ten minutes in order for the glue to have time to set.

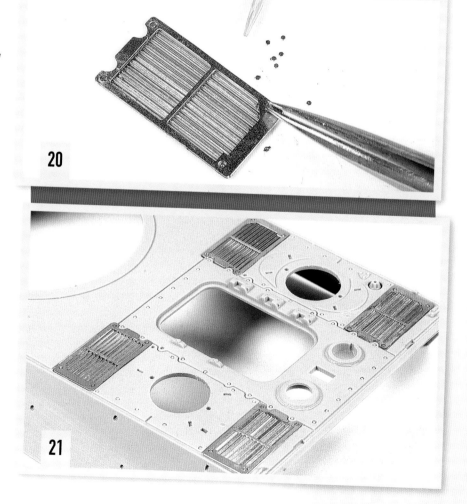

PHOTO 22 AND 23:

Lets look at a few other tips for soldering PE parts. Sometimes it is easier to solder parts while they are still attached to the fret such as what I did with the rods that mount these Tiger I exhaust guards. After attaching the rods I clipped them to length, cut the parts from the fret, and glued the bolts onto the opposite side.

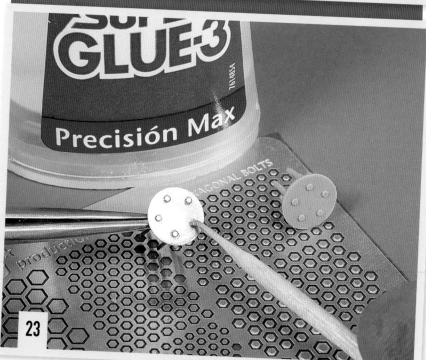

PHOTO 24 AND 25:

Takk and Blu-Tack can aid in securing parts freeing up your hands during soldering or gluing fine details. Takk is a little more rigid than Blu-Tack and was designed for this purpose.

PHOTO 26 AND 27:
Today there are a number of turned aluminum gun barrels on the market from a variety of different manufacturers. They are all rather inexpensive and can save time as no seams need to be removed or do any gaps need to be filled after assembly. I have found that both the dimensions and diameters of these aftermarket items can vary. I would recommend doing some research prior to purchasing one if you are a stickler for detail. Some of these guns have fine brass parts that can be tricky to assemble. You can align these parts inside of the muzzle breaks and carefully glue them with the aid of a tapered round file.

Now that we have discussed the basics of assembling brass and other metallic parts let's move onto a more complex Tiger I stowage bin. It is on these large complex assemblies that the strong bonds from soldering become much more important.

SOLDERING COMPLEX PHOTO-ETCH ASSEMBLIES

COMPLEX PHOTO ETCHED ASSEMBLIES CAN BE WELL WORTH THE EXTRA EFFORT IF YOU KNOW HOW TO GET THE MOST OUT OF THEM.

This Tiger I turret stowage bin was built to be placed onto a veteran tank. I wanted it to be like the rest of the other large components on this vehicle containing damage. I would not have bothered spending the extra time on this detail otherwise. Although I enjoy soldering photo-etch I seldom undertake involved assemblies unless I plan on adding some effects that will add both character and originality to the finished model. Let's now look at some of the techniques needed to assemble an involved project such as this.

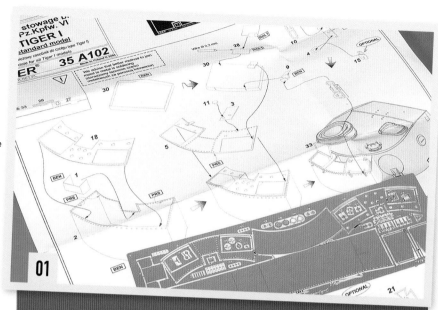

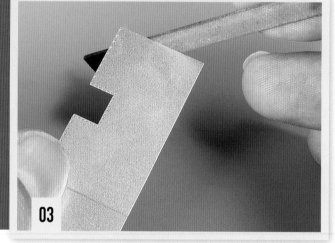

PHOTO 1 THROUGH 3:
You could save yourself some problems and time if you first study the instructions. Sometimes it is easier to first make sub-assemblies or even solder parts together while they are still on the sprue. Assembling parts like this can be difficult so plan carefully. I decided to start with the large parts of the bin first.

PHOTO 4:
There are a number of rivets on the exterior that need to be pushed out from the inside prior to assembly.

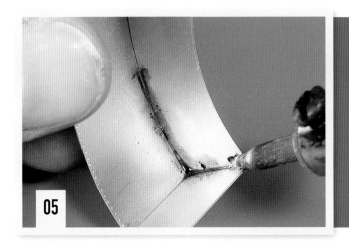

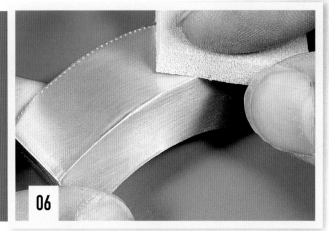

PHOTO 5 AND 6:

Simply use your fingers when forming large parts. Solder the parts from the inside to keep the exterior clean and professional looking. This is a good tip to remember if you publish articles or place photos of your unpainted work on webpages. Use sanding sponges and other polishing tools to clean the exterior.

PHOTO 7 THROUGH 9:

There are two layers at the top of the bin. I had some difficulties fitting the inner layer (part number 18). In this case I decided to start from one side and work my way around the outer edges. If you are quick when applying solder to parts containing lots of soldered joints you shouldn't have any problems with the other pieces coming loose. I accidently made a small dent on the exterior of one of the openings. These mistakes happen. It probably would not have been too apparent on the completed model. In the end I simply decided to add a dent to this area.

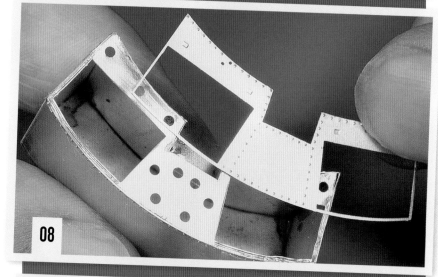

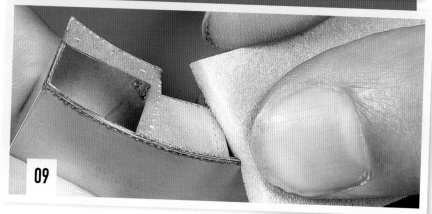

10

PHOTO 10 THROUGH 14:
I started forming the hinges by first making a 10 degree bend in the parts with the aid of a bending tool. A piece of wire was used to finish forming the hinges. Next I soldered the wire in place, slid on the other part of the hinge, and cut it to size.

11

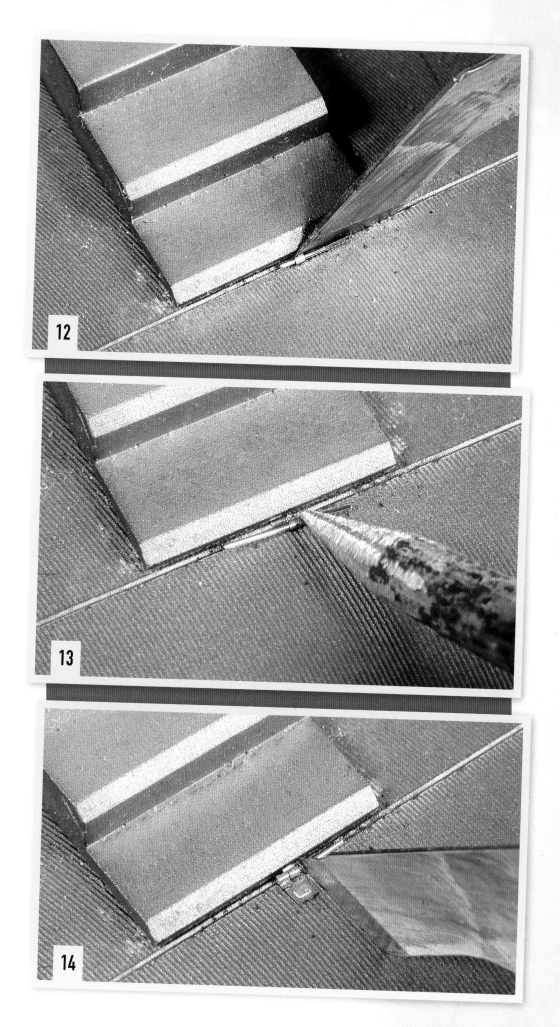

PHOTO 15 THROUGH 17:
I decided to attach the hinges onto the door prior to soldering the finished assembly onto the body.

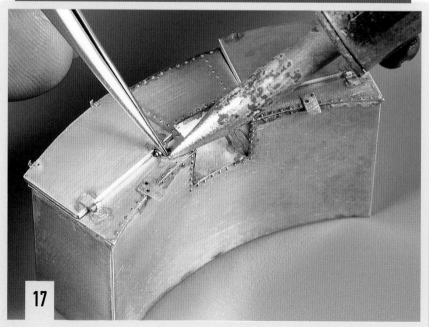

PHOTO 18 THROUGH 21:

I started making the small arms impacts using a pointed scribing tool. Holes where then placed on the dents using a drill. I placed a small round file inside each of the holes and rotated it to widen them just a bit..

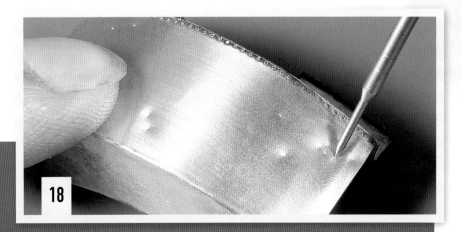

PHOTO 22 THROUGH 24:

The most difficult parts on these larger assemblies are always the smallest details. Soldering small parts together while one is still attached to the fret can sometime be much easier. You are less likely to lose small parts this way. I finished the stowage bin by attaching the fine parts and bolts using superglue. A pin vice and a fine piece of stretched sprue where used to deposit the superglue.

This dented turret bin, full of bullet holes, adds a lot of authenticity to the finished model. There are literally hundreds of photo-etched kits on the market and they will all need different techniques to properly assemble them. I would also recommend that you start with the more easy, larger parts and move forward from there. Another metallic medium available is copper and brass sheet.

Copper and brass sheet can sometimes help you obtain effects when photo-etched sets are not available. Let's now look at an example.

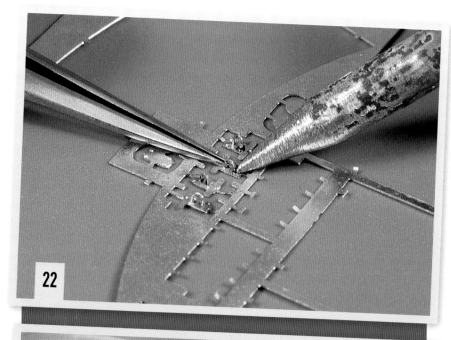

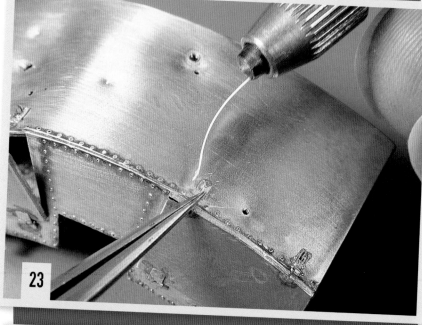

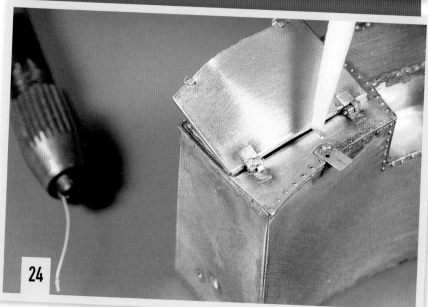

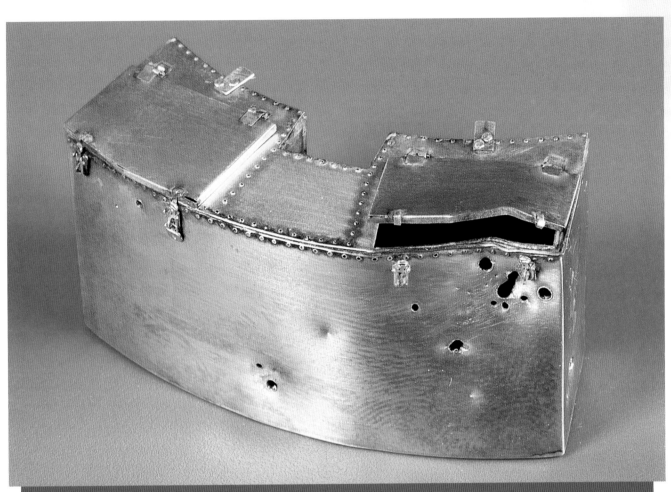

SCRATCH-BUILDING PARTS FROM COPPER SHEET

01

PHOTO ETCHED BRASS PARTS ARE A GREAT MEANS FOR CREATING REALISTIC BATTLE DAMAGE.

Despite the numerous sets of photo etch there will sometimes be those cases when what you need is not available. The bed spring armour on this theoretical JS-3 depicted during the battle for Berlin was one of those exceptions. Here we can also see how copper sheet can be very handy in replacing plastic details to create realistic battle damage.

The base of this replica was the Tamiya JS-3 kit. There are a few brass sets and accessories for this model. These sets are not designed for completely recreating the sheet metal sides in the way I had envisaged. Again, this was to be a veteran tank that has seen difficult combat. These light-guage metal sides

covering the inverted sloped plates would contain numerous dents and bullet holes. I could not create these same effects in the moulded plastic of the Tamiya kit. I also wanted to create some mattress armour protecting both the lower, and parts of the upper hull. Mattress armour is just a general term that has been given to field-fabricated stand-off armour used by most of the armies during the Second World War.

You can buy sheets of copper and brass in different guages at most art and craft stores. Most of the copper that I have seen comes in rolls. Copper is more ductile than brass and easier to form. It can also be soldered like brass.

PHOTO 1 AND 2:
The mattress armour along with the new metal side that I constructed for this model are fairly basic. Below are most of the tools needed to get started. Numerous straight edges and squares were also required for the scribing of straight lines ensuring proper cuts.

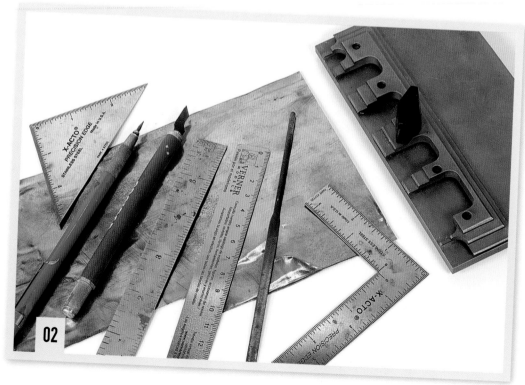

02

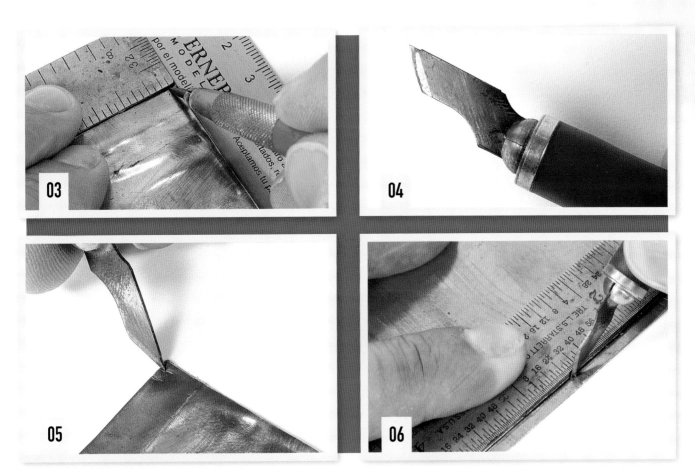

PHOTO 3 THROUGH 6:

I started constructing the frames of the mattress armour first. Two straight-edges were used to help me mark the copper at 1/16" (1.5mm) intervals. I usually use a no. 24 X-acto blade to help me mark and scribe copper sheet. I made small indents on each of the marks that would be easier to see over the light pencil marks. Next, I lined up the straight-edge to the indents at each side and scribed a good line into the copper with a few stiff slices using the hobby knife.

PHOTO 7 THROUGH 9:

I lined up the scribed mark firmly in the jaws of my bending tool and bent it back and forth until the strip broke free as seen in photo 8. I repeated these steps a number of times until I had about six even strips of copper. All of the burs where cleaned using a file and pliers.

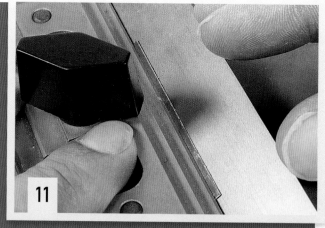

PHOTO 10 THROUGH 12:
After cutting the strips to length I pressed marks on the centers at each side. These marks would allow for ease of alignment in the bending tool allowing me to place a bend into each of the strips. Press a rigid straight-edge over the bend after forming to help insure a 90 degree angle.

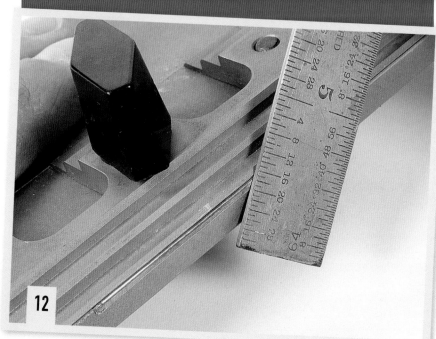

PHOTO 13:
I used a square edge to help guarantee that the frames would have 90 degree corners once soldered.

PHOTO 14 THROUGH 17:

The screens used were a brass product from K & S Engineering. These delicate details need to be cut carefully. Keep making light passes over the screen with the aid of a straight edge letting the weight of the knife cut the material. You will only tear the screen if you press too hard. I soldered the screens to the frames at regular intervals.

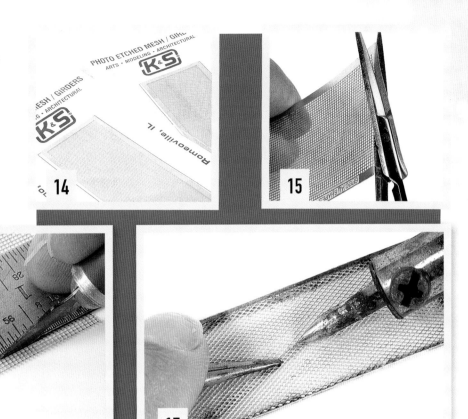

PHOTO 18 THROUGH 21:

I wanted the mounts for the mattress armour to be a bit sturdier. Also available on the market are brass structural shapes. They come in all types of different forms and sizes and are real handy to have. The larger section seen in photo 21 was used to help keep the upper part, being held by the tweezers, flat on the lower section ensuring a good joint for soldering.

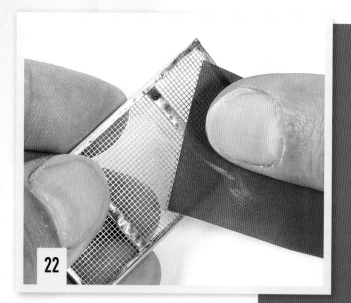

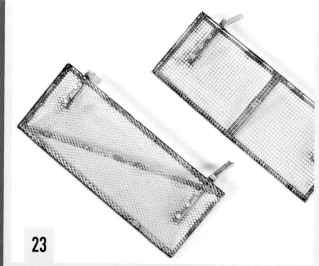

PHOTO 22 THROUGH 24:
Once assembled, I polished the brass frames with fine sandpaper making them look professional. Bolts and washers were horded from a spare PE set I had lying around. I randomly placed some dents into the frames and screens with the aid of a rigid straight edge.

PHOTO 25 AND 26:
I always feel better if large brass assemblies like this are fastened well to the plastic. I soldered brass rods onto the lower sections of the frames that would be attached to the upper turret and hull. I then slid these rods into holes that I drilled into the plastic. Attaching the frames in this manner would allow me to remove the frames for painting once the assembled model was photographed. They would also allow for a stronger bond when glued after the model was completed.

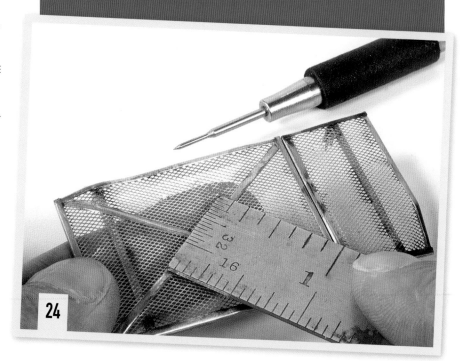

PHOTO 27 THROUGH 32:
The metal assembly on the side of the JS-3 was cut using the same methods discussed earlier. When possible, I would strongly recommend first fabricating replacement parts prior to cutting up the model. This way you will have a reference helping to ensure proper dimensions. Dents and small arms impacts were also added prior to placing the assembly onto the model. The final step was to firmly solder the frames for the mattress armour onto the new copper side of the JS-3.

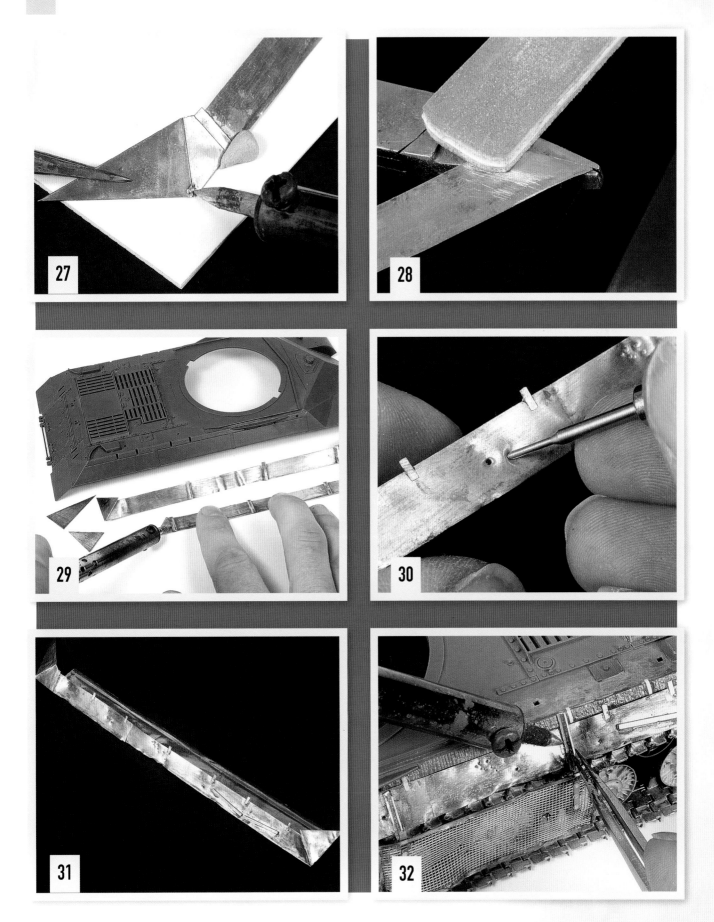

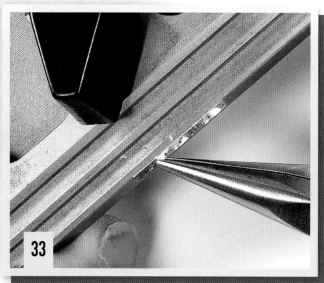

33

34

35

36

PHOTO 33 THROUGH 38:
There were a few parts from some PE sets that I had for the JS-3 which could be used in conjunction with the new copper side adding further detail and authenticity. These parts were also dented prior to being glued into place. Sometimes the superglue will dry slowly when trying to attach PE parts onto a model. Holding the part in place while brushing accelerator over the fresh glue can help to solve this problem.

I ran into some problems with the fabricated copper side on this subject. To my dismay I found that it can easily be broken free do to the limited areas where I fixed it using super glue. I should have soldered some rods onto the inside of this detail to be placed onto holes in the plastic for added strength like on the upper hull and turret mattress armour. When properly assembled, as seen in the photos, I found all of the extra work well worth the final appearance. Again, you can see how a bit of imagination and added effort can completely change the look of

any familiar subject such as this before you even start painting it.

The E-50 is another example of using copper sheet to make my own features in order to enhance the Trumpeter kit that is rather limited in detail. The same techniques used to create the copper details on the JS-3 were also employed to fabricate the cylindrical exhausts, spare track mounts and field-installed side skirts.

37

38

PHOTO 39 THROUGH 42:
To rebuild the exhaust I first made a cylinder and placed a small amount of solder at each end with the aid of a rolling tool. After I removed the cylinder from the tool I finished soldering it, then sanded the built up solder smooth again with the aid of the rolling tool.

PHOTO 43 THROUGH 45:

I carefully removed the pipe from a spare Panther G exhaust and glued it onto the new copper cylinder. A thin disk of evergreen plastic tubing was glued to the inside of the cylinder to aid in firmly attaching the elbow using plastic cement. Once more you can see that taking a bit of time to replace plastic details with copper ones can allow you to create realistic looking damage.

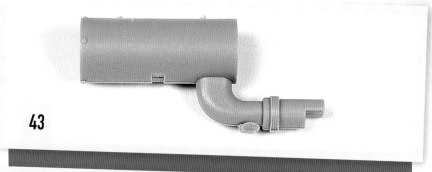

43

44

45

PHOTO 46 THROUGH 48:

When using your imagination to create copper details from scratch first look around at some of the existing photo-etched kits available. Parts from this Panther A set of side skirts were used to help me create the field installed mounts on the E-50. Photo-etch sets like this are not to too expensive when you think of the time that might have been needed to create some of those fine parts from scratch. Let's now look at a bit about preparing photo-etch and other metal parts for painting.

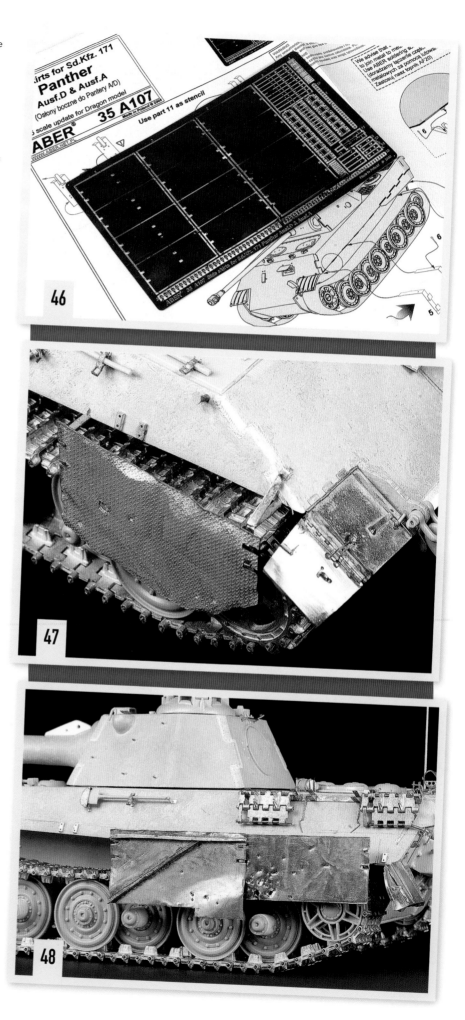

The damage on this JS-3M would be very difficult to duplicate without the mediums and methods discussed in this chapter. Being able to recreate this damage would make a scale replica of this tank much more interesting and lifelike.

PREPARATION FOR PAINTING

LIKE WITH PLASTIC I WOULD RECOMMEND GENTLY CLEANING SOLDERED BRASS PARTS IMMEDIATELY AFTER ASSEMBLY USING DISHWASHING DETERGENT AND AN OLD SOFT BRISTLED TOOTHBRUSH.

PHOTO 1:

Cleaning the parts will remove fluxes and oils that might affect the coats of paint. Depending on the type of flux along with the heat used in the soldering process, photo-etched brass will tarnish over time forming fine textures that might be evident through the base coat. Priming the photo-etched parts quickly upon finishing the model will reduce this problem. Prior to priming the parts I strongly recommend photographing the model if you are planning to publish the work. Assembled models with shiny brass parts look much more attractive then when they are covered in a dull, matt grey primer.

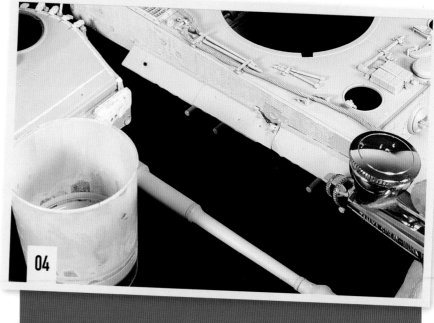

PHOTO 2 AND 3:

I often use Tamiya primer from a can. It adheres fairly well onto metal parts. It can be sprayed straight from the can with good results. I like to first spray Tamiya primer into a cup then thin it just a bit further using a few drops of lacquer thinner.

PHOTO 4 THROUGH 7:

I only lightly prime the metal parts on the model therefore airbrushing the primer gives me much more control of its coverage.

You do not need to completely cover the parts using primer. Just two to three light coats are all that you will need. I usually do not prime the plastic parts of a model. Most paints, including acrylic types, on the market adhere fairly well to plastic. An additional coat of primer under a basecoat might also cover fine details so try to apply it only where needed.

06

07

CONCLUSION

YOU SHOULD BEGIN FORMULATING A GOOD IDEA OF HOW YOU ARE GOING TO PAINT THE MODEL WHEN YOU ARE CONSTRUCTING IT.

The basics covered in the different parts of the JSU-152 build example are the most important and will help to make your model more authentic and also more competitive in the contests if you choose to enter them.

In the next book we will cover the different painting phases and techniques again starting with the basics such as the importance of applying a good basecoat. Then we will move on to some of the more technical and even controversial methods such as using hairspray along with speckling and colour modulation.

With friends at the FNSS Military Land Vehicle model competition.

The presentation of awards at the Meng exhibit during the 2014 Bajing Hobby Fair in China with David Parker, Brett Green and Kristof Pulinckx.